The Complete Synthesizer

EXCLUSIVE DISTRIBUTORS:
BOOK SALES LIMITED
78 NEWMAN STREET, LONDON W1P 3LA, ENGLAND
THE PUBLISHERS
...NEY, NSW 2064, AUSTRALIA

...HT 1982 BY
...LES LIMITED)
...V1P 3LA, ENGLAND

... PART OF THIS BOOK MAY BE
...RONIC OR MECHANICAL MEANS
...ORAGE AND RETRIEVAL SYSTEMS,
...WRITING FROM THE PUBLISHER
...MAY QUOTE BRIEF PASSAGES IN A REVIEW

...6
...1649

...OMBIE
...BELL
... DESIGN CONSULTANTS
...& JOHN DOWNS
...OD SHONE
...6,87,92,94,95,96 & 97: DAVE CROMBIE
...RCUITS PROPHET X
...KEYBOARDS)

... BY:
...LONDON & BECCLES

SS
EY/COLOGNE

P.S. 52024

PREFACE

The aim of this book is to familiarize the reader with the fundamentals of electronic music and, in particular, the workings of the electronic music synthesizer. Although this book caters for the person with little or no knowledge about synthesizers, more experienced "synthesists" will discover useful technical and background information, and will thus find this is a most useful reference source.

Those with less experience of synthesizers will soon get to grips with what is, essentially, a fairly simple subject to comprehend. Once the basic principles have been grasped, then all the subsequent information and technicalities will fall neatly into place. It is for this reason that the novice should, initially, work through this book in the order in which it is laid out. Little advantage will be gained by jumping ahead to more advanced subjects: the old analogy of requiring firm foundations on which to build still holds true, even in the relatively new world of electronic music synthesis.

Towards the end of the book is a Glossary of Terms, which you may find particularly useful to refer to whilst in the earlier chapters of the book. Explaining the workings of the synthesizer can become something of a "chicken and egg" problem, so the glossary can be of great benefit. Additionally, it will serve as a useful source of information in the future.

If some form of electronic music synthesizer is on hand whilst you are reading, it will make understanding the various points being covered a lot simpler, (i.e. if they can be "tried out" on an instrument). Obviously, not all synthesizers are the same, and some instruments won't be capable of performing all the functions dealt with, but it will still be most worthwhile to study this book in conjunction with a synthesizer, if possible. Don't worry if you haven't got such an instrument; you will still find the subject easy to follow. However, your appetite will probably be whetted to such an extent by the time you've read the book that you will want to get your own synthesizer. If this does become the case, then you will be well-equipped with the information required to help you decide which particular synthesizer will best suit your requirements.

When dealing with a topic of this nature, most authors start by looking at the history of the subject, outlining the various advances made over the years. In this instance, it would seem most appropriate to examine the principles and functioning of the synthesizer first, before dealing with the past advances which have resulted in the present state of things. In this way, the reader will be better able to grasp the importance and the relevance of particular discoveries and inventions, and to see how these developments have shaped the instruments of today.

The synthesizer itself is often considered to be the "be all and end all" by certain technical buffs. However, it must be remembered that the synthesizer is a *bona fide* musical instrument; it is not a machine, but a tool with which to create music.

It is possible for almost anyone to use this tool, but, unless they fully understand the basics of its operation, they will find it hard to produce exactly what they want. With the aid of this book, you will see a whole new area of music opening before you. The rest is up to you.

CONTENTS

INTRODUCTION

"What is a synthesizer?"

One of the most asked questions regarding this topic is, "What exactly is an electronic music synthesizer?". The answer, quite often, isn't forthcoming. At this stage, a synthesizer can best be defined as a device that constructs a sound by determining, uniquely, the fundamental elements of pitch, timbre, and loudness. Now, a synthesizer isn't a synthesizer, full stop: there are many different types of this instrument. It isn't a product like a motor car, where various models all perform more or less the same function. There are three possible prime routes to take when producing a "synthesizer" sound; then there are different categories of each of these three classes of synthesizer; then further divisions and types. And that's before we get to considering the actual models of instruments themselves. Look at the family tree **(figure 1)** of all the various possible types of instrument: there are a lot, aren't there? So, the possible permutations of the way in which a sound can be synthesized – what type of synthesis do I need to use? monophonic or polyphonic? – are considerable. When the exact type of instrument needed has been decided on, only then can I look around and see what models are available.

But don't be put off – things aren't as confusing as they might at first seem. You see, the majority of synthesizers available today – especially those in the lower price bracket – are based on the principle known as subtractive synthesis. We don't have to worry too much at present about the other two groups. However, as technology is advancing, more and more of these other machines are appearing, and becoming less expensive. We will be looking at them in detail in due course. At present, it is sufficient to realize that, if someone goes into a music store and asks for "a synthesizer", it is as if they were to go into a greengrocer's and ask for "some vegetables."

But why has the synthesizer appeared only relatively recently on the musical instrument map, and why is it now enjoying such popularity? You may also ask why a book of this nature is indeed necessary. As Chapter 6 will confirm, the idea of the synthesizer isn't a new one. Almost since the advent of electrical devices, inventors have been designing musical instruments using the then "new technology" to create sounds from individual analysis of the three elements – pitch, timbre, and loudness. The big breakthrough came with the advent of the transistor, and, more recently, the integrated circuit and micro-computer. As with the development of all mechanical and electrical items, the technology of the day dictates the nature and cost of the available product. The synthesizer is no different: its present existence is a direct result of today's advanced electronic technology.

The 1970's saw the transition of the synthesizer from a box of tricks, meticulously built by hand in an inventor's small back-street workshop, to a multi-million-pound industry, with huge companies, such as Yamaha and Roland, investing small fortunes in research and development to stay one jump ahead of the field.

The synthesizer is, to some extent, a universal instrument. It is often thought to be specifically a keyboard instrument, but this doesn't have to be the case. Over recent years, there have been guitar synthesizers, drum and percussion synthesizers, and even wind synthesizers: all these instruments rely on the same basic principles of operation, it is just the control medium that is different. The keyboard has come to be the most widely-used

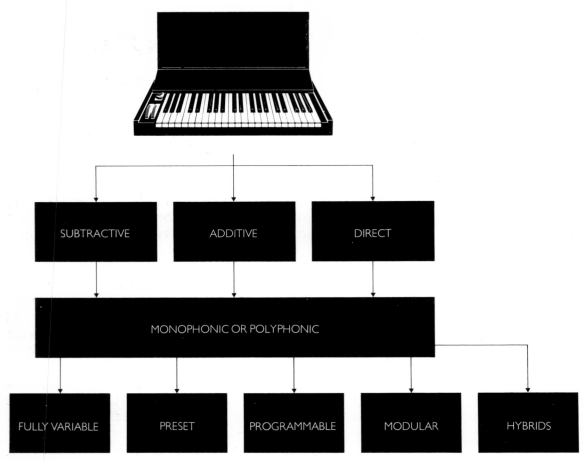

FIGURE 1: PART OF THE SYNTHESIZER MAKE-UP.

controller for two prime reasons: first, it is particularly suitable for interfacing with the electronic circuitry of the synthesizer – it is, basically, only a series of switches arranged in a row; second, the keyboard has been shown to be the most efficient way in which to "feed" information into an instrument, especially when playing polyphonically, (i.e. more than one note at a time).

The heart of the majority of electronic music synthesizers is the voice module. It is with this collection of circuits that the pitch, timbre, and loudness parameters are determined and shaped. The voice module is essentially the same basic design for keyboard, guitar and wind synths, it is just the control mechanisms that are different, so this book will be of use not only to keyboard players, but also to other musicians wanting to enter this world of electronic music.

1
UNDERSTANDING SOUND

As the voice module is so important to the workings of the synthesizer, it is necessary to understand the workings and reasonings behind this device. However, to grasp fully the concepts involved, we must first go back and look at the very nature of sound. There is little point in learning how to operate a tool without first studying the job for which it is intended. For this reason, this chapter is devoted to the physics of sound.

WHAT IS SOUND?

Sound is the sensation that we experience when movement or vibrations in the air are detected by our ears. Our ear converts these vibrations into information signals which are transmitted to the brain, where they are decoded and translated into what is our concept of sound.

How is sound transmitted through the air?

The air all around us is made up of microscopic particles which are used to transmit the information that makes up a sound. You may remember the school physics lab experiment used to illustrate this fact: a bell is placed inside a sealed jar, and all the air gradually pumped out. As the air is being removed, the bell's ringing becomes increasingly faint, until it is almost inaudible. In space, there is no air, and the sound will not be carried; however, water, which is a more efficient transmitter, will carry a sound much further.

If we consider a mass of air in which no sound is being carried, we will find that the particles have more or less a uniform density: there will obviously be movement in the air, but there will be nothing that our ears can detect. Let's now bring a drum into our mass of air and give it a fair old biff with a stick – look what happens in **figure 2. 2a** shows the random particles around the drum; as the drum is struck **(2b),** the skin is stretched and the particles just above the skin suddenly find that they are occupying a much larger volume – i.e. there are the same number of particles, but they are occupying a much larger space, the enlarging being caused by the downward movement of the drum skin. This is known as rarefaction. The tensioning of the skin of the drum causes the stick to bounce off, and, at the same time, the drum-skin springs outwards **(2c),** causing the particles that had been rarefied now to be compressed. The skin will continue to oscillate backwards and forwards **(2d,e,f)** until it settles back into its initial position: the time it takes to do this depends on various things – the tensioning of the skin, the damping, how hard the drum was hit, and so on.

Look now at the particles above the drum's skin. In **2b,** we saw the particles undergoing rarefaction, then, in **2c,** they were compressed. In the meantime, the rarefaction has been passed on to particles above the new compression and, in **2d,** we can see the way in which the vibrations in the air are starting to be transmitted. It must be realized that the individual air particles themselves are not travelling away from the skin of the drum; they are just moving backward and forward (see the particle marked by a cross): it is the compressions and rarefactions that are being transmitted, and are moving away from the source. In a synthesizer, sound is produced indirectly. Electrical vibrations are set up in the circuitry, and these are then amplified and fed to a loudspeaker, the cone of which, acting like our drum, causes the electrical vibration to be translated into sound waves.

FIGURE 2: THE EFFECT ON THE SURROUNDING AIR PARTICLES OF STRIKING A DRUM.

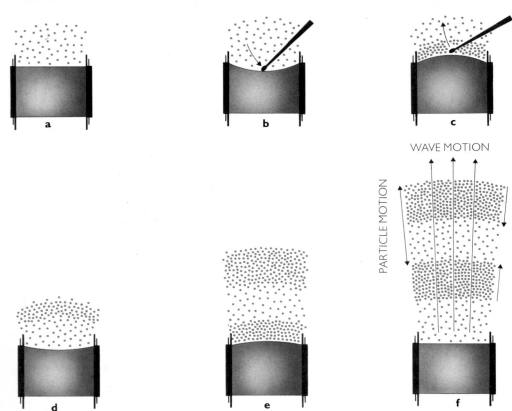

THE THREE ELEMENTS OF SOUND

When we hear a sound, it can be defined at any one instant by considering three different parameters: the pitch; the timbre (from the French word for tone colour); and loudness, or amplitude. Things aren't quite as simple as that, as a sound might be emanating from more than one source, for example, an orchestra, whence it would be necessary to make a composite analysis; however, it is sufficient to say that a single sound can be defined by these three prime parameters.

PITCH

The pitch of a sound is that quality which makes it seem higher or lower than other sounds. The notes at the top or right-hand end of a piano are pitched higher than those at the bottom or left-hand end. The pitch of a note is determined by the rate at which vibrations are set up in the air particles, i.e. the rate at which compressions and rarefactions take place.

Let's now consider the effect on the air particles of a vibrating tuning fork. When such a device is struck on a hard surface, the prongs vibrate back and forward at a predetermined rate – you can see this by holding the vibrating fork up to the light, and seeing that the prongs appear blurred. In **figure 3,** we can see that, as the prongs move outwards, the air particles are compressed and, when they move back inwards, the air is rarefied. As the tuning fork produces compressions and rarefactions in the air at a fixed rate, waves of particle vibrations

FIGURE 3: AIR PARTICLE VIBRATIONS CAUSED BY A TUNING FORK.

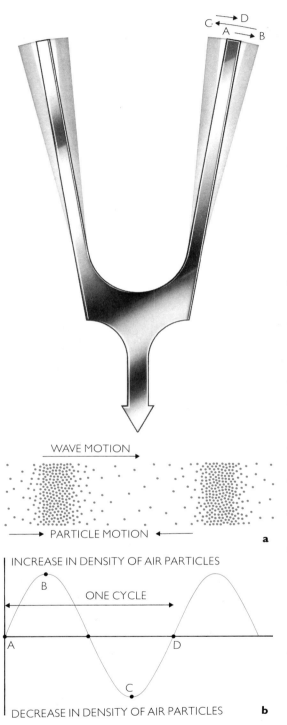

WAVE MOTION

→ PARTICLE MOTION ←

a

INCREASE IN DENSITY OF AIR PARTICLES

ONE CYCLE

DECREASE IN DENSITY OF AIR PARTICLES

b

are set up in the air surrounding the fork. These waves move away from the fork at the speed of sound. In air, this rate approximates 330 metres per second (around 700 miles per hour). However, the figure varies, depending on the density of the air, and its temperature. **Figure 3** shows this particle motion and the emanation of the waves. If we now illustrate graphically the changes in density of the air particles caused by the disturbances from the prongs of the tuning fork, we end up with a plot as shown in **figure 3b.**

The line running through the centre of the plot is the mean density of the air, i.e. how the air particles would look if there were no vibrations being caused. The higher up the density scale the plot goes, the greater the compression of the air particles: when it falls beneath the line, the air particles are rarefied. It can be seen that the shape of the plot produced is regular: the vibrating prongs set up a series of shapes known as sine waves. These are very important to the theory of the synthesizer, and we shall be dealing with these many times throughout the book. As the waves move away from the source (the prongs) at a fixed rate (the speed of sound), the length of each sine wave is dependent on the rate at which the fork's prongs vibrate. A single cycle of a sine wave is shown in figure **3b**, from point A to point D. This can be considered to be the changes in the air set up by the prongs of the fork moving from centre position A out to B, in to C, and back to centre position D(A) one complete cycle.

The distance that a wave covers in the time it takes to complete one cycle is known as the wavelength, and the number of cycles that are made each second is known as the frequency. However, as previously mentioned, the speed at which the wave moves through the air (V) is fixed, so there is a direct relationship between the wavelength (λ), and the frequency (f). $\lambda = V/f$, i.e. the length of a cycle equals the distance in which the sound travels in one second, divided by the number of cycles of that sound, occurring in that second.

A low frequency sound will have a long waveform and a low pitch. The higher the frequency, the shorter the waveform, and the higher the pitch.

STANDARD TUNING

When several musical instruments are being played together in a group, quartet, orchestra, or whatever, it is necessary – in order to preserve not only musical but also physical harmony – to tune all the instruments so that they are in the same pitch. That is to say, when the same note is played by all the instruments, they will all be producing waves with the same number of cycles per second. In order to simplify matters, a tuning standard has been established which, in the Western world, requires that an instrument sounding the note 'A' should be producing a waveform with 440 cycles every second (or even multiples thereof). It is for this reason that you will encounter tuning forks (the simplest way to produce a fixed standard pitch) marked A-440. The unit of frequency, cycles per second, is often known as Hertz (or Hz).

THE RESPONSE OF THE HUMAN EAR

There is a limit to the range of frequencies that can be detected by the human ear. This range varies considerably from person to person, depending primarily on age, but also on other variations – health, job conditions, and the like. The lower threshold (the frequencies beneath which we cannot discern audibly the vibration of the air particles) is generally between 18 and 25 Hz. The ear can detect frequencies up to about 20,000 Hz (or 20 kilohertz), though, as we get older, this figure can fall off quite rapidly. The range of human hearing is often known as the **audible frequency spectrum.**

FREQUENCY AND MUSIC

We shan't go too deeply into the theory of this subject here, as it is more the domain of the musical harmony books. However, it is important to grasp the way in which pitch and frequency relate to the structure of conventional Western music.

The octave is the most important concept to grasp in terms of the use of the synthesizer. If we consider our standard tuning pitch A-440, where the sound is vibrating, or oscillating, 440 times every second, then the A one octave above will vibrate 880 times a second, and the A an octave below will vibrate at 220 Hz. So, for every octave rise in pitch, the frequency doubles.

Most musical scale systems are based on the octave. However, different civilizations divide the scale up in many different ways. We shall concern ourselves with the Western twelve tone scale, but, even having decided thus, the octave can still be divided up in several ways – there is the system of just intonation, whereby the octave is divided into notes that are not equally spaced, though they do bear a very close relationship, harmonically, to one another. The violin, being a fretless instrument, is capable of playing just intervals and this scale does sound particularly pleasing to the ear; however, when played in ensemble with fixed tuning instruments, such as the organ or piano, the effect is somewhat less pleasing!

As will soon become apparent, the equally-tempered scale is almost universally used in electronic music (though a small number of synthesizers can be programmed to play a just scale). This is primarily due to the way in which the instrument functions (see Chapter 2). In this scale system, the octave is divided into twelve equal parts, so, in **figure 4,** we can see how the scale of C is made up.

TIMBRE

Timbre is the quality of a sound that enables the listener to distinguish that sound from another of the same pitch. The timbre, or tone colour, of a note depends on the actual shape of the waveform produced. If we go back to our example of the sine wave produced by the vibrating tuning fork, we see how the compressions and rarefactions of the air determine the shape of the waveform produced. Look now at the configuration of the particles in **figure 5.** The source of the sound is such that the particles are compressed to a certain pressure for a certain period of time, and then rarefied for an equal period. **Figure 5b** shows the graphical representation of this vibration. This waveform is known as a square wave. The wave still travels at the same speed as for the sine wave, so, if it is of the same wavelength, the ear will interpret its pitch as being the same; however, because the air particles are vibrating in a different manner, the ear will perceive its sound to have a totally different tonal colour.

Unlike pitch, there is no simple quantitive measurement of timbre. The only way to express this parameter is to describe the wave form produced. This is all very well for simple shapes, such as the two we've already mention ed, but, since just a small variation in the shape of a waveform can make a considerable difference to the timbre the ear perceives, then a more satisfactory way of describing this parameter is necessary.

Any waveshape can be described mathematically; however, the maths involved would, to most of us, be far too complicated to work out, and, to a large degree, the exercise would be pretty worthless. There is another way, however, which is particularly important when using additive synthesis for constructing sounds. This relates to the harmonic structure of sound and is dealt with more fully in ADDITIVE AND SUBTRACTIVE SYNTHESIS.

FIGURE 4: COMPARISON OF FREQUENCIES BETWEEN JUST AND EQUAL SCALINGS.

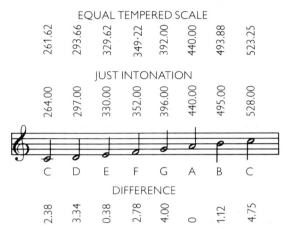

EQUAL TEMPERED SCALE							
261.62	293.66	329.62	349.22	392.00	440.00	493.88	523.25

JUST INTONATION							
264.00	297.00	330.00	352.00	396.00	440.00	495.00	528.00

| C | D | E | F | G | A | B | C |

DIFFERENCE							
2.38	3.34	0.38	2.78	4.00	0	1.12	4.75

FIGURE 5: RAREFACTIONS AND COMPRESSIONS CAUSED BY A SQUARE WAVE.

a

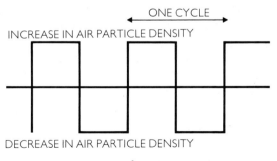

ONE CYCLE

INCREASE IN AIR PARTICLE DENSITY

DECREASE IN AIR PARTICLE DENSITY

b

LOUDNESS

On the surface, the concept of loudness is a much simpler one to grasp. If we consider our sine wave example again, then the more the air particles are compressed and rarefied, the greater will be the peaks and troughs of the sound wave, and the ear will detect that the sound produced is much louder. Now, the ear behaves in a rather strange manner to different levels of sound – it doesn't respond in a linear fashion. This means that a waveform with twice the amplitude won't sound twice as loud to the ear. Another anomaly concerning perceived loudness involves the timbre of the sound: a brighter tone will sound louder than a pure simple one, for example a sine wave.

Because the ear doesn't respond in a linear manner, loudness is normally measured in decibels. This is a ratio of two values whereby a sound is compared to a reference level. Normally this reference point is considered to be the threshold of hearing – that is, a sound level that is only just perceptible. On this scaling, live rock music has a rating of around 90 to 120 dB, whilst a transistor radio, in an average sized room, would be operating at around 50 dB. Clearly, the transistor radio isn't putting out a signal equivalent to half that heard at a rock concert.

When considering the loudness of a sound, the dynamics (or changes in loudness) are a vital aspect. Listen to the sound produced by playing a note on a piano. As the hammer strikes the strings the output of the piano rises from nothing to a maximum level almost instantaneously, the sound then starts to die away gradually as the vibration of the strings is damped by the air. The note is then released, causing the piano's dampers to deaden the strings, and the note dies away fairly rapidly till all is quiet again. During the course of this note, the loudness, or amplitude, has been continually changing: the shape of the loudness of the note is known as the envelope, and this is a most important concept – so much so, that, when synthesizing a sound, the envelope often plays a more vital part in creating the overall effect than does the timbre.

PERIODIC AND APERIODIC WAVESHAPES

There are two distinct types of waveforms: periodic and aperiodic. Periodic waveforms have a repetitive pattern, as in our earlier example of the waveform produced by the tuning fork. The pattern can, of course, be as complicated as necessary; however, there would come a point when the pattern would repeat itself, i.e. a new cycle would start. Over a longer period of time, the shape of the wave may change, but, essentially, each cycle would be almost identical to the preceding one.

An aperiodic waveform is a "one-off", the most obvious example being the envelope waveshape as discussed in the previous section. These waveforms occur only once, and, consequently, have no pitch. There are other examples of aperiodic waveforms which are audible: the sounds produced by waves crashing on a beach, or by rain hitting the ground. However, the waveforms produced by these phenomena are so complex that there is no discernible repetitive pattern.

ADDITIVE AND SUBTRACTIVE SYNTHESIS

We are now in a position to examine more closely the two most important types of synthesis: additive and subtractive. Let's look firstly at additive synthesis.

The sine wave that we encountered when using the tuning fork is considered to be the fundamental waveshape. It cannot be broken down into any simpler format. However, it is possible, by adding together sine waves of different frequencies and amplitudes, to create any other waveform. The lowest, or root, of these sine waves is known as the fundamental, and the other sine waves that are used to construct the sound are known as the overtones. Most acoustic sounds tend to have overtones that bear a direct mathematical relationship to the fundamental, and, hence, to one another. These overtones are known as harmonics.

RESONANCE

If we move off at what might appear a tangent, let's look at what happens when ringing a church bell. Here we are concerned with the way in which the rope is pulled, not the sound produced. In order to get a very heavy bell rocking backwards and forwards, with the minimum of effort, it is necessary to pull on the rope at certain moments in time. Every time the rope is pulled, an additional amount of energy is fed to the bell to build up its swing. When something vibrates at its own natural frequency (which, in the case of our rocking church bell, would probably be in the order of once every four seconds – 0.25 Hz) as a result of being acted upon by another force at the same frequency, it is said to resonate, and the natural rate at which it vibrates is known as the resonant frequency. If you try to make the bell rock faster, you will find that a considerable amount of effort will be needed to break the natural rhythm of the rocking. However, it is possible to pull on the rope at half the natural frequency, i.e. once for every two swings of the bell, or every three times, and so on, and the bell will still rock at its natural frequency, but with proportionately less amount of swing.

Another example of resonance can be shown by tapping your teeth with a pencil. When you do this, the sound produced has a definite pitch: this pitch is determined by the resonant frequency of the cavity of your mouth; by changing its shape, it is possible to alter the pitch of the sound.

We now come to what is known as the natural harmonic series. If we stay with our tuning standard of note middle A vibrating at 440 cycles/second, then let's take our fundamental sine wave to be two octaves below this note, at A-110 (f=110 Hz). This is the fundamental, or first harmonic. Now, as we have seen, most sounds are made up of a fundamental tone, which gives the sound its pitch, and a series of related harmonics. These harmonics are simply multiples of the fundamental frequency: in our example the second harmonic would be a frequency of 220 Hz (2 × f), the third harmonic would be at 330 Hz (3 × f), the fourth harmonic 440 Hz, and so on. So, most sounds can be expressed as a fundamental, and a series of harmonics: it is the relative amplitudes of these harmonics that distinguish one sound from another. It is possible to illustrate how a series of related sine waves (fundamental and

FIGURE 6:
ADDITION OF ODD HARMONICS IN PROPORTIONAL AMOUNTS TO GIVE A SQUARE WAVE.

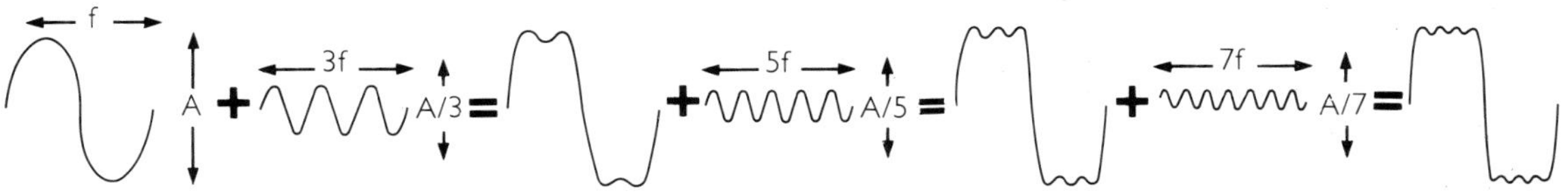

harmonics) can be used to generate another waveform. **Figure 6** shows how a square wave can be constructed by adding together odd harmonics (F, 3, 5 …) in certain proportions. If we start by adding together the fundamental and the third harmonic in an amplitude ratio of 1:3 (i.e. the third harmonic is a third of the fundamental's level), then we get the waveshape shown on the right-hand side of the diagram. If the fifth harmonic is then added, in a ratio of 1:5, then we get a waveform that is starting to look like a square wave. The seventh harmonic is then added, and so on: with each additional harmonic, the square wave gets more and more "square" – the corners get sharper. It can be seen, therefore, that a square wave contains harmonic elements that can be of very high frequencies.

For example, the eleventh harmonic, although only one eleventh the amplitude of the fundamental, is at 1210 Hz (11 × 110 Hz).

The usual way in which to illustrate the harmonic structure of a waveform is to draw a harmonic spectrum diagram. **Figure 7** shows the make-up of the square wave. It isn't necessary to specify the pitch of the square wave, as the harmonic series is related to the fundamental, the frequency of which is immaterial. Similarly, the amplitudes of the harmonics do not have to be given set values: again, it is the relative amplitude with respect to the fundamental that is important.

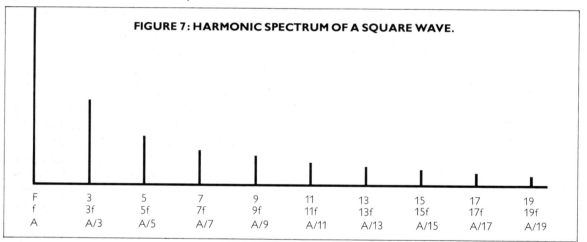

FIGURE 7: HARMONIC SPECTRUM OF A SQUARE WAVE.

F	3	5	7	9	11	13	15	17	19
f	3f	5f	7f	9f	11f	13f	15f	17f	19f
A	A/3	A/5	A/7	A/9	A/11	A/13	A/15	A/17	A/19

WAVEFORMS

When considering a waveform, the frequency is not important. A square, or for that matter any waveform, can be vibrating at half a cycle per second, 100 cycles per second, or a million: it is still the same waveform. At this stage, however, we are primarily interested in the waveforms that fall within the audible frequency spectrum, though, in synthesis, similar waveforms are also used outside this range for modulation and tone generation purposes (see chapter 2). The most common geometric waveforms are the square wave, sine wave, rectangular wave, sawtooth, and triangle.

THE SQUARE WAVE

Although the sine wave is considered to be the fundamental element, when it comes to producing this waveform electronically, the task is somewhat more tricky. Strangely enough, it is the square wave that is the simplest waveform to produce electronically. A square wave, as can be clearly seen from its shape, exists only in two states – "high" and "low". In electronic terms, this can be translated to a circuit being switched on or off. In fact, the action of flicking a light switch on and off can be said to produce a square wave. If we were to listen to a pure square wave of around 400 Hz, we would hear a mellow, hollow-sounding tone, somewhat reminiscent of the sound of a woodwind instrument. In fact, the similarities between the harmonic series of the square wave, and that of a clarinet are quite striking. If a section of a sustained clarinet note were analyzed, the harmonic

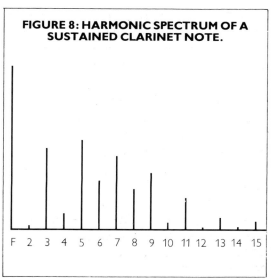

FIGURE 8: HARMONIC SPECTRUM OF A SUSTAINED CLARINET NOTE.

content of the signal would look something like that shown in **figure 8.** Note how closely this corresponds to the harmonic series of the square wave, with the odd harmonics (first, third, fifth etc.) most prominent.

THE RECTANGULAR, OR PULSE WAVE

This is a variation on the square wave. Again, the waveform exists in just two states: high and low. However, unlike the square, the period of the cycle for which the waveform is high differs from the time it is in a low state. The way in which this is defined is known as the duty cycle. **Figure 9** shows rectangular waves with varying duty cycles. If we take one complete cycle as 100%, then we can express rectangular waves in terms of a percentage – a 40% wave would be high for 4/10ths of the cycle and low for 6/10ths. When considering a rectangular wave within the audible frequency spectrum, it doesn't make any difference to the perceived sound if the duty cycle is 40% or 60%: the waveform has just been inverted, and its harmonic content remains the same. The audible pulse wave has a reedy, nasal quality, though, of course, the sound produced depends on the value of the duty cycle.

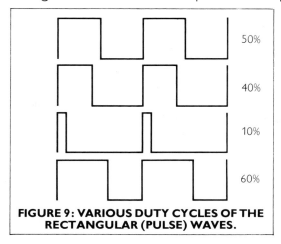

FIGURE 9: VARIOUS DUTY CYCLES OF THE RECTANGULAR (PULSE) WAVES.

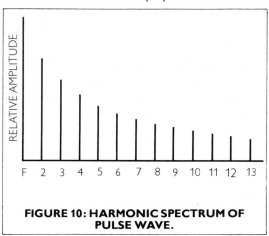

FIGURE 10: HARMONIC SPECTRUM OF PULSE WAVE.

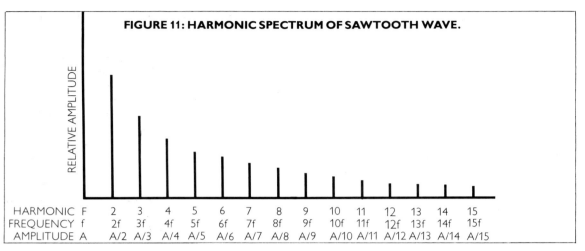

FIGURE 11: HARMONIC SPECTRUM OF SAWTOOTH WAVE.

HARMONIC	F	2	3	4	5	6	7	8	9	10	11	12	13	14	15
FREQUENCY	f	2f	3f	4f	5f	6f	7f	8f	9f	10f	11f	12f	13f	14f	15f
AMPLITUDE	A	A/2	A/3	A/4	A/5	A/6	A/7	A/8	A/9	A/10	A/11	A/12	A/13	A/14	A/15

THE SAWTOOTH WAVE

The sawtooth wave, also often known as the ramp wave, is like the pulse wave formed by the addition of all the harmonics. However, this time, the relative amounts are different. As can be seen from the diagram, the amplitude of the higher harmonics falls away considerably more quickly than for the pulse wave. This is reflected in the shape of the wave. The sharper the edges of the waveform, the greater the higher harmonic content. The audible sawtooth wave has a brassy quality to it. It is a very full-sounding waveform.

THE TRIANGLE WAVE

It can be seen that the triangle wave is similar to a sine wave, but with the edges flattened, and, consequently, points at the peaks and troughs. Its harmonic content is, therefore, very heavily weighted in favour of the fundamental, but with a harmonic consisting, like the square wave, of odd harmonics. However, the attenuation of these harmonics is very rapid, so that the ratio of the eleventh harmonic to the fundamental is 1:121 (the relative amplitude of the nth harmonic being $1/n{\times}n$).

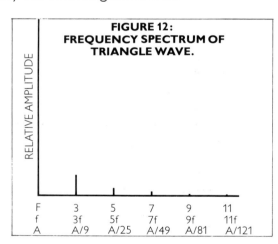

FIGURE 12: FREQUENCY SPECTRUM OF TRIANGLE WAVE.

F	3	5	7	9	11
f	3f	5f	7f	9f	11f
A	A/9	A/25	A/49	A/81	A/121

OVERTONES

There are some tones that cannot be created by adding together multiples of the fundamental tone. Most notably, these are clangorous sounds – ones that are created by striking metallic instruments, such as gongs, bells and glockenspiels. The overtones produced by these instruments do normally have a relationship with the fundamental frequency. It isn't, however, a straight multiple; more often, these overtones have frequencies of the order of 13/4, or 9/2 (say) the fundamental frequency. It is often the case with some of these percussive instruments that the fundamental frequency itself is almost impossible to determine.

FIGURE 13: MUSICAL RELATIONSHIP BETWEEN HARMONICS OF VARIOUS WAVEFORMS.

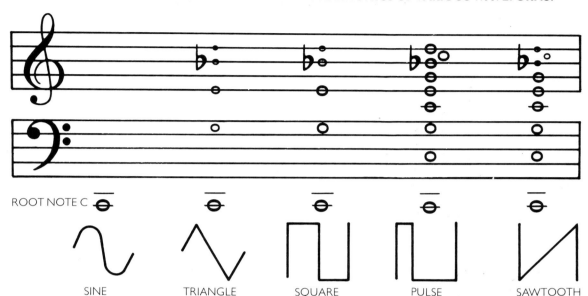

We now come to the first fork in the road – the sound created by additive or subtractive synthesis. Additive synthesis is the construction of a sound by adding together varying proportions of fundamental and harmonic sine waves (and sometimes overtones) to produce the desired sound.

Subtractive synthesis utilizes a suitable waveform that is rich in harmonics, filtering the unwanted part of the signal out, to leave only the desired signal.

When employing additive synthesis, it is necessary to have a considerable number of sine wave generators at one's disposal. As the harmonic content of most sounds is continually varying, it is necessary to be able to change the relative amplitude of each of the harmonic sine waves continually (i.e. each sine wave has to have a separate amplitude envelope). This results in rather a lot of complex control circuitry, and, consequently, instruments that are of the additive ilk are normally computer-based and fairly expensive.

The subtractive method of tone generation, although more restricted, is considerably easier to control and certainly less expensive. It is for these reasons that the subtractive synthesizer has become the most commonly found type, devices known as oscillators producing the waveforms, whilst the filter(s) remove the unwanted parts of the signal. The filter is, in many respects, analogous to the body of a guitar, or the soundboard of a piano, in that it gives the instrument a particular tone colour.

2
THE SYNTHESIZER VOICE MODULE

INTRODUCTION

In this chapter, we are looking at the workings of the synthesizer using the subtractive principles, as discussed in Chapter 1.

The synthesizer voice module is at the heart of every subtractive synthesizer, although it may not always be apparent. Many of the controls mentioned may not appear on the front panels of these instruments, but the majority of the features mentioned will be present in most instruments.

The three elements that define a sound – the pitch, the timbre and the loudness – are primarily determined by devices known respectively as oscillators, filters, and amplifiers . The signal is generated by the oscillator, then fed through one or more filters so that the timbre of the sound may be shaped, and then passed through an amplifier in order that the sound may be given some dynamics (change in loudness). It then passes out of the instrument and into a basic audio amplifier and speaker arrangement. So, the signal flow is from oscillator, to filter, to amplifier, and out. And this is the basic composition of a synthesizer voice module.

At this stage, it is simplest if we adopt the "building block" approach and illustrate the voice module as it appears in **figure 14**. In addition to the three main blocks, there are three others: a low frequency oscillator (LFO), and one or two envelope generators. The LFO is used to modulate the pitch of the oscillator, and the envelope generators produce aperiodic (non-cyclic) waveforms that shape the amplitude of the note (dynamics), and can alter the timbre of the signal during the course of the note.

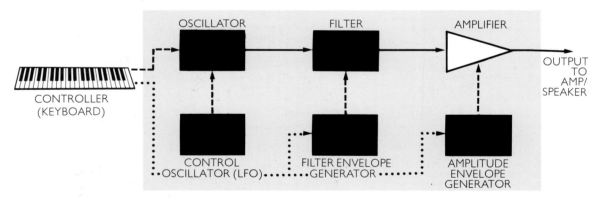

FIGURE 14: THE BASIC SYNTHESIZER VOICE MODULE CONFIGURATION.

VOLTAGE CONTROL

Voltage control, when used in conjunction with an electronic music synthesizer, is like having a third, fourth, or even fifth hand. The synthesist uses voltages to do most of his work. The three blocks, already discussed, are voltage-controlled; the voltage controlled oscillator (VCO) generates a different pitch depending on the voltage that is applied to it. The voltage controlled filter will remove certain parts of the signal, again determined by the voltage applied to it. And, similarly, the voltage controlled amplifier changes the loudness of the output in amounts proportional to the voltage applied to it. But what exactly is a voltage?

A voltage is a difference in electrical potential. Simple household batteries provide a voltage between their two terminals. This is a steady fixed voltage (d.c., or direct current) used to power various devices. This d.c. voltage can be compared to a tank of water situated high above the ground, with the electrical potential between the two battery terminals equivalent to the distance between the tank and the ground. Connecting up the battery is like letting loose the water from the top, where, because of its potential energy (i.e. height), it can do some work on its fall down to ground: it can turn a generator, for example. The higher the tank of water, the more work it can do. Similarly, the more electrical potential there is between the two terminals of the battery, the greater the power, and, hence, the voltage, of the battery. A changing voltage is equivalent to a change in pressure caused by moving the water up and down.

In a synthesizer, the control voltage is used not to power the circuitry (although there is obviously some electrical power being applied to make the circuit work), but to govern certain parameters. For example, let's consider the voltage controlled oscillator. The greater the voltage applied to its input, the faster it will oscillate. Now, the VCO isn't taking all the power of the voltage to make it go faster; it is looking to see how great the voltage applied to it is, and adjusting its rate of oscillation accordingly. In our water tank example, it is analogous to there being a device that measures how high the tank is above the ground, which then feeds this information to the relevant device (i.e. the VCO) in order to get the correct response.

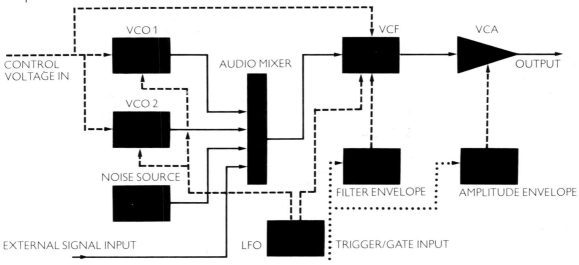

FIGURE 15: TYPICAL SYNTHESIZER VOICE MODULE SHOWING HARD-WIRED SIGNAL FLOW.

The beauty of using a voltage controlled system is that the outputs from each block – the oscillators, the envelope generators, the low frequency oscillators, et al – are all voltages, and can, therefore, be used to automatically control another parameter.

Most synthesizer voice modules are "hard-wired" to a set pattern, so that only certain control block configurations can be set up. **Figure 15** represents a typical synthesizer voice module and the various hard-wired signal routings. Note that, here, we have two oscillators and a noise source as the signal generators, and that the relative amount of each of these signals is determined by an audio mixer.

In this representation of the voice module, there is one signal output, but in order to get this output, there have to be two pieces of information fed into the voice module: the module has to be told what note is being played, and when it has to sound. These are the only two pieces of information that are vital, though extra data relating to how a note is played can be utilized by some synthesizers, and, as in this case, there is a facility for processing an external signal.

THE CONTROLLER

The "identity" of the note being played is conveyed to the oscillator(s) as a control voltage, so, quite simply, the higher the control voltage, the higher the oscillator's pitch will sound. In order to tell the voice module when and for how long the note is to sound, a signal known as a gate pulse is used. The only two blocks that need to know when the note should start and finish are the envelope generators (some synthesizers have only one of these devices). It is the job of the controller (usually, though not always, a keyboard) to supply this information to the voice module. The controller is not considered as part of the synthesizer voice module. The voltage controlled oscillator receives a voltage signal from the controller and it is important that it responds to this signal in the correct manner. It is for this reason that most synthesizers use the convention of "one volt per octave" – that is to say for every one volt increase in the signal from the controller, the frequency of the oscillator doubles (rises by one octave). Let us take as our controller a basic keyboard, as shown in **figure 16.** If the bottom note is played (C), no voltage is produced; however, if the next C up is depressed, the voltage generated will be one volt exactly. The next C up will produce two volts, the next three volts, and so on. Going back down to the bottom octave and depressing C-sharp will produce a voltage of 1/12 volt: why? The answer is simple: the octave is divided into twelve equal parts (the equally tempered scale, see chapter 1), so each semitone we move up the scale will result in a rise of 1/12 volt.

FIGURE 16: CONTROL VOLTAGE OUTPUTS FROM THE KEYBOARD.

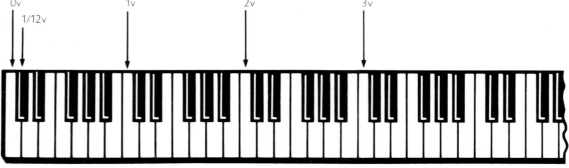

Not all synthesizers use the "one volt per octave" system. Some manufacturers prefer to adopt a linear scale, whereby the frequency rises 1000 Hz (say) for every one volt rise in the control voltage. In this instance, the control voltage would have to be scaled logarithmically (unequally) in order that the correct musical intervals be maintained.

THE GATE PULSE

As with many new industries, standardization of particular control signals is slow to happen. However, there seems to be a distinct move at the moment towards what is known as a positive going gate pulse. The gate is simply a signal that the controller sends to the synthesizer voice module to tell it when a note is being played and for how long. Closely associated with the gate is another similar signal, known as the trigger pulse. **Figure 17** clarifies the differences between these two pulses. A gate or trigger pulse (like a square or rectangular wave) can exist in two states – "high" and "low", or "on" and "off". If we consider a keyboard again as our controller, every time a key is depressed, a switch is closed and a pulse produced. This pulse is of a fixed voltage, normally between five and ten volts, depending on the make of the synthesizer. The trigger pulse is of fixed length, generally in the order of a twentieth of a second (but, again, varying with the model), and occurs the instant the note is played, so all it can do is tell the voice module that a new note has been played. The gate pulse is a far more useful signal, as it is open-ended. When a key is played, the gate pulse goes high (switches on) and stays high until the key is released. In this way, an extra piece of information is passed to the synthesizer voice module: namely, how long the note is sustained.

So, why bother with a trigger pulse at all? Most controllers generate just a gate pulse (and, of course, the control voltage), and the internal circuitry of the synthesizer voice module can detect from that exactly when a new note is played. However, there are instances when it is useful to have both a trigger and a gate signal separately available, as we shall see later on.

There are other types of actual gate and trigger "pulses". Some manufacturers employ the "short to ground" pulse, which means that when a key is depressed, carrying this signal becomes short-circuited to ground for the duration of the "pulse".

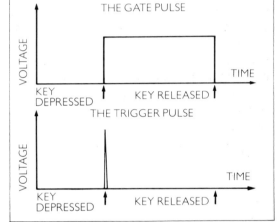

FIGURE 17: GATE AND TRIGGER PULSES.

THE GATE PULSE

VOLTAGE / TIME / KEY DEPRESSED / KEY RELEASED

THE TRIGGER PULSE

VOLTAGE / TIME / KEY DEPRESSED / KEY RELEASED

Ground is equivalent to Earth on a mains socket. The advantage of this system is that several "pulse" sources can be connected together (for example, the controller and a footswitch), and it only needs one of them to be activated for the synthesizer voice module to respond.

This subject is discussed in further detail in the sections dealing with monophonic and polyphonic keyboards.

THE VOLTAGE CONTROLLED OSCILLATOR

The voltage controlled oscillator can be said to consist of three sections: the voltage summer; the oscillator proper; and the wave shaper.

The VCO receives control signals from:
    a – The controller, telling it the pitch of the note played (control);
    b – The front panel controls, which set the fine tuning of the oscillator (fixed);
    c – The low frequency oscillator for possible modulation – this is used to give the output
        frequency a vibrato or trill effect (periodic);
    d – A possible external control voltage for bending the pitch of the note using a footpedal
        (control).

All these control voltages are added together in various amounts in order to produce a single composite voltage. This is then fed to the oscillator which produces a tone whose pitch is proportional to the voltage. In order to create the desired waveforms, a waveshaper is used to convert the tone into the various waveforms (sine, sawtooth, square, rectangular, triangle, etc.), though the pitch will remain constant. This is, in essence, the work performed by the VCO.

Strictly speaking, the VCO has a hand in determining the timbre of the final sound, as well as the pitch, as it is responsible for shaping the waveforms that are to be subsequently filtered. However, the major part of the tone shaping is performed by the voltage controlled filter.

We dealt with the main geometric waveforms that are to be encountered in most synthesizer voice modules, but this isn't the end of the story with regard to the tone generation side of things. To be honest, the output from a single oscillator doesn't sound particularly exciting: the tone seems very flat (not tuning-wise, I must add). No naturally occurring sound is pure and continuous, so, in order to inject a degree of "life" into the proceedings, the synthesizer designers deemed it would be better to have more than one oscillator for each voice. Many voice modules do consist of only one VCO; however, the more versatile, and, consequently, more expensive instruments normally consist of more than one audio oscillator.

PHASE

In order to understand the benefits that two or more oscillators bring to a synthesizer, it is necessary to introduce the concept of phase. **Figure 18** shows two triangle waves that

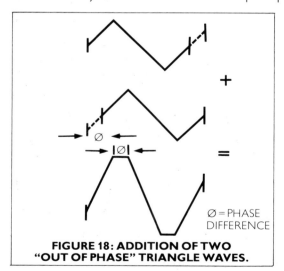

Ø = PHASE DIFFERENCE

FIGURE 18: ADDITION OF TWO "OUT OF PHASE" TRIANGLE WAVES.

have exactly the same wavelength and amplitude; however, they start their cycles at different times – the second wave lags a bit behind the first. If we were to listen to these sounds, our ears couldn't distinguish between them – they both have the same pitch and timbre. However, if the two were to sound at the same time, then we would notice a difference. Look at the resulting waveform when the two triangle waves are added together: the tops have been flattened and a new waveform produced. This will have a different timbre to the original sawtooth wave, and, consequently, a different harmonic structure. The two triangle waves are said to be out of phase with one another, and the

24

difference between the two waveforms is known as the phase angle, Ø. Notice that, if the two waveforms are half a cycle out of phase with one another, and of the same amplitude, they will cancel one another out! When a synthesizer voice module incorporates two VCO's, their output waveforms are not phase related: there is no physical link between the oscillators. The only common element is the control voltage being applied to each oscillator and this determines the pitch – the phase is independent. So, if we were to tune two VCO's to the same pitch, and add (mix) together their output waveforms, assuming they are the same shape and amplitude, then we would expect to get a steady waveform much like that in **figure 18** (though the exact shape would depend on the value of the phase angle). Well, in reality, this *isn't* the case. Unless an effect known as synchronization (qv. synchronization) is utilized, the two waveforms will never be exactly in tune with one another. They may be only fractionally out, such that the human ear could not detect if the VCO's were heard separately, but they will not be exactly in tune, which, surprisingly enough, is a good thing. Before finding out exactly what is going on diagrammatically, consider a grand piano. It has, in the main part, three strings for every note: what's wrong with one? A twelve string guitar has strings arranged in pairs – why? If you play a note on a piano whilst damping two of the strings, you'll hear why three are used. Similarly, if you compare the sound of a twelve-string acoustic guitar to a six-string, you'll notice the difference. When two or more free phase signal generators are played in unison, the quality of the sound is enriched way out of proportion to one's expectations. This is all due to the various generators, strings and the like not being perfectly in tune with one another; consequently, the phase angle between them is continuously changing.

Figure 19 shows this effect. Unlike the example in **figure 18,** there is a difference in the tuning between the two waveforms, such that VCO 1 is oscillating at 10 Hz, and VCO 2 at 11 Hz (say). It is necessary, for diagrammatic reasons, to consider these oscillations to be at such a low frequency; if we were to depict the effect at audio levels, the figure would stretch off the page and a couple of yards out to the right! It doesn't matter that we are considering sub-audio waveforms: the resulting effect holds true for vibrations at any frequency. So, if we add together our two triangle waves of 10 Hz and 11 Hz, we get a very

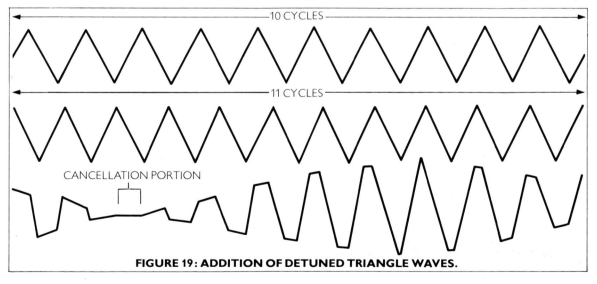

FIGURE 19: ADDITION OF DETUNED TRIANGLE WAVES.

strange-looking waveform. On closer examination, though, it can be seen to be a periodic wave with a cycle lasting exactly one second. This is known as the beat frequency, and, for two oscillators with frequencies close to one another, its value will always be the difference between the two pitches.

The phenomenon of the beat frequency isn't just applicable to synthesizer theory: it is the most useful aid to anyone tuning an instrument. For example, the piano tuner will start by tuning a certain note until it is pitched exactly the same as his reference tuning fork. He does this by adjusting the tensioning in the string until there are no beats to be heard when the fork and string sound simultaneously. If the beat frequency is zero cycles per second, then the two pitches must be the same. It is possible, once one note of a piano has been tuned, to complete the job for the entire instrument using beats. The job is fairly long and requires a lot of patience, but it can be done.

Returning to our dual oscillator voice module, we can now see how a changing phase angle can inject extra depth into the tones produced by these oscillators. However, if, as shown in **figure 19,** the two oscillators are producing signals of almost identical waveforms, and almost in unison with one another, the effect of cancellation will become a problem. This could mean that you would be playing a solo, and the amplitude of the signal would momentarily fall away to nothing. The best results, when using two oscillators nearly in unison, are obtained by having them running between 2 and 5 Hz apart. If you detune them any further, unwanted sideband frequencies are introduced and these will destroy the natural harmonic relationships already present.

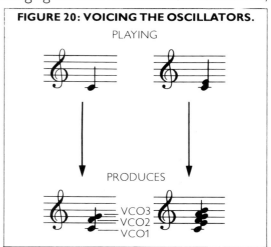

FIGURE 20: VOICING THE OSCILLATORS.

PLAYING

PRODUCES

VCO3
VCO2
VCO1

Another advantage of having more than one oscillator is that they can be set up with a predetermined interval between them. For example, oscillator 2 could be set an octave above oscillator 1: this would give a fuller tonal characteristic to the sound. Taking things a bit further, if we had a three oscillator voice module, VCO 2 could be set a fourth above VCO 1, and VCO 3 could be set a fifth above VCO 1, so (as illustrated in **figure 20**) by playing a C on the keyboard (controller), the notes C, F, and G would sound. This produces a really full rich sound. Great care must be taken, however, if you are using a tuning such as this with more than one voice module (i.e. a polyphonic synthesizer), as it is very easy to play a chord that will set up a dissonance between the fourth and fifth components of the different voice modules. It is seldom necessary, however, to set up an oscillator tuning of this complexity.

THE SINGLE OSCILLATOR VOICE MODULE

We mentioned in the last section that a single tone on its own doesn't sound particularly exciting, and that two or more oscillators considerably widen the horizons for the synthesist. However, that doesn't mean that synthesizers that have just a single VCO (or, in the case of polyphonics, a single VCO per voice) cannot produce rich full sounds. There are two "devices" that designers utilize in order to fatten up the sound of the single oscillator synth, and it is often the case that dual oscillator voice modules also incorporate these features.

THE SUB-OCTAVE SQUARE WAVE

This is the simplest, and cheapest, way for the synthesizer designer to enable the voice module to produce a fuller sound. It simply consists of a square wave that oscillates exactly one octave below the frequency of the VCO. It is produced by halving the VCO's frequency, and generating a hi-low (square) waveform, and is, consequently, phase related to the main VCO output. **Figure 21** shows the two waveforms and their fixed phase relationship to one another.

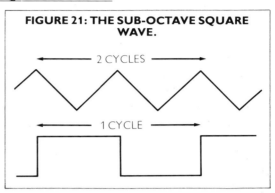

FIGURE 21: THE SUB-OCTAVE SQUARE WAVE.

PULSE WIDTH MODULATION

This is a particularly useful feature of both the single and the dual oscillator voice module; however, it isn't always to be found. When the signals from the two oscillators running almost in unison **(figure 19)** were added together, the resulting waveform "moved" as a result of the beat frequency induced. **Figure 22** shows a similar state of affairs, but this time using square waves. Notice how the resulting waveform looks like it consists of a series of pulses with continuously changing widths. It is possible, as we have seen, to produce an oscillator output with a pulse shape, and it is a simple matter for that pulse's duty cycle to be adjusted so that high – low proportions (i.e. the pulse width) can be adjusted as required. If we twiddle the pulse width control knob as a note is being played, it is possible to get a crude simulation of the dual oscillator "unison" sound. However, this isn't a very satisfactory situation; not

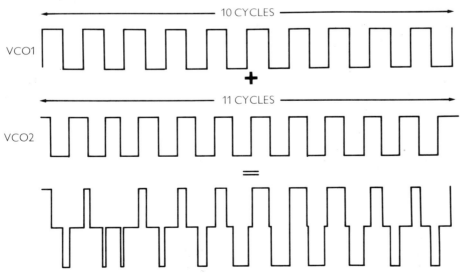

FIGURE 22: ADDITION OF TWO DETUNED SQUARE WAVES.

27

only will our fingers become tired of twiddling one knob backwards and forwards, but also the effect will be rather ragged and jerky. So, we need a way of automatically varying the pulse width of a signal, and that's what pulse width modulation does.

If we take a sine or triangle waveform that is oscillating at, say, one cycle per second – 1Hz. (Low Frequency Oscillator), and then use it to vary the width of the pulse (rectangular) wave produced by the VCO, we get a waveform as depicted in **figure 23.** Again, the VCO waveform has been drawn at 10 Hz in order to fit on the page, but it can be seen that this modulated waveform bears some resemblance to the resultant of the two square waves running at 10 Hz and 11 Hz. It is not identical, but the quality of the sound produced (when considering waves in the audio spectrum) is fairly similar. You can, therefore, create a fairly rich moving sound with just one VCO and a low frequency oscillator, the frequency of which corresponds to the beat frequency when using two VCO's.

The obvious disadvantage of this system over the dual oscillators is that you are confined to a single waveform. With two VCO's, it is possible to "beat" sawtooth waves with triangle waves, square waves with triangle waves, and so on, and you therefore have a much wider range of possible tones. However, the pulse width modulation principle does work, and will produce a pleasant moving sound, and should be considered a "must" for the single oscillator synthesizer.

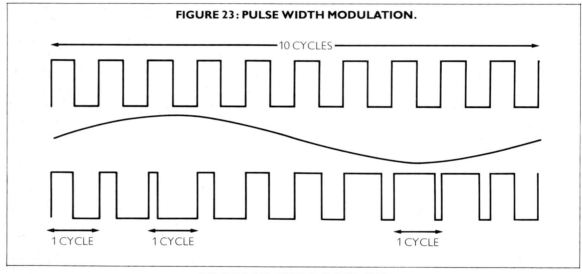

FIGURE 23: PULSE WIDTH MODULATION.

THE NOISE SOURCE

In Chapter 1 we discussed periodic and aperiodic sounds. So far, all the audio signals produced by the synthesizer voice module have been periodic, consisting of cyclic waveforms. In order that the synthesizer may simulate some of the aperiodic sounds – wind, thunder, waves, as well as a range of other non-natural voicings – there has to be some form of random signal incorporated into the voice module. This is known as the noise source, and is essentially a signal made up of all the frequencies across the audio spectrum lumped together with varying amplitudes, such that the result is a hissing sound that has no trace of any pitch. The sound is similar to that produced by a VHF radio tuner when off-station.

There are two main types of noise that are encountered when dealing with electronic music. First, white noise, which has an equal spread of frequencies right across the audio spectrum: this has the hissing quality described above. Often a synthesizer voice module will have a source marked just "noise", and this will generally refer to a white noise source. The second kind is known as pink noise, and is somewhat softer sounding, as it tends to be biased towards frequencies at the lower end of the spectrum, (i.e. it has had some of the high frequencies attenuated, or filtered).

For the more mathematically minded, the biasing of the frequencies for white and pink noise can be described as follows. There are more whole number frequencies in each octave the higher up the audio spectrum you consider: between A-220 and A-440 (one octave), there are 220 different frequencies, whereas between A-880 and A-1760, there are 880 frequencies. It therefore follows that white noise, consisting of frequencies balanced across the entire audio spectrum, will tend to sound more of the upper frequencies than pink noise, which consists of frequencies producing equal amounts of energy per octave; consequently, a frequency towards the top end of the audio spectrum will play less of a part than one in a lower octave.

In subtractive synthesis, a noise source is generally used as a starting point, and is further modified to produce the desired effect. On its own, a noise source is not a lot of use, save that it can be used as an audio mask. If you are in a room, and you want all external sounds to be made inaudible, a noise source will act to blot out all other noises. This can be easily demonstrated. Tune your radio in between VHF stations to provide a noise source. Put on a pair of non-isolating headphones, and then ask someone else in the room to talk to you: you will find it almost impossible to hear them. However, if you tune to a radio station at comparable, or even higher, level, you should now be able to hear what they are saying fairly easily. White noise is therefore a useful tool in the more horrifying business of sensory deprivation. The synthesizer is the only instrument whose playing could literally be described as torturous.

AUDIO MIXER

We have dealt with all the prime signal sources. It is now necessary to combine them into a single signal that is then passed on to the filters and amplifiers. In order to combine the signals, an audio mixer is employed. This is a very simple device and, in many cases, isn't even identified as such. It consists basically of a set of volume controls from each of the sound sources. In a single oscillator voice module, it isn't normally necessary to have separate volume controls, but just a balance control between the noise source and the VCO. However, when, as in some cases, there is no noise source, no such control is necessary. In many synthesizer voice modules, a balance control is provided for balancing between the two oscillators, and there's a second control for setting the noise level. This is fine for most applications, where all that is important is the relative balance between the various signal sources. However, if the voice module(s) should form part of a programmable instrument, then it is important to have separate control either of each individual source, or over the final output amplitude (see Chapter 3).

It is at this stage that any external signal is normally fed into the voice module as a possible sound source. This is combined with all the other signals, and becomes part of the composite sound fed to the filter.

A TYPICAL SIGNAL GENERATOR BANK

Before moving on to the next section, it would be as well to consider a typical bank of signal generator controls, just to visualize exactly how all the theory so far mentioned relates to an actual synthesizer.

Figure 24 shows the controls of a typical dual oscillator bank. The Master Tune adjusts the fine tuning of both oscillators around three semitones: this is so that the synthesizer can be simply tuned to other instruments. VCO 1 has four rotary controls: the Range control sets the oscillator in one of the five footage registers, thirty-two being the deepest, two the highest. This would be a five-position rotary switch. The waveform selector, again a rotary switch, has four positions, so that VCO 1 can provide either a sine, triangle, sawtooth or rectangular wave. In this last position, the two controls marked duty cycle and pulse width modulation (PWM) amount come into play. If the duty cycle is at 50%, a perfect square wave is produced; reducing the cycle causes the duty cycle to become less balanced, until, at 5%, a very narrow pulse indeed is being produced. The PWM amount control introduces a degree of width modulation about the setting of the duty cycle; therefore, if the duty cycle were set at 50%, a smooth chorus-like modulation effect would be created. However, if the rectangular wave was set at 5%, the effect of the width modulation would be to narrow the pulse even more so that the signal would disappear completely for part of the cycle. This can be put to good use, especially for creating echo-like effects.

VCO 2 is similar to VCO 1; however, there is a frequency control that can be used to transpose the pitch of the output by any part of an octave. This is used so that intervals (for example, a fifth) can be set up between the two oscillators. Note that there is no frequency control for Oscillator 1, as it is always going to remain pitched as the fundamental, or root note. The Range control of VCO 2 has an extra position marked "Lo", which enables it to be set in the sub-audio frequencies, and can therefore be used as a modulating signal itself. A switch marked "Kbd Track – on/off" is used in conjunction with the "Lo" range position, in order that the control voltage from the keyboard, or other controller, need not change the rate of low frequency oscillation of VCO 2. This is important if this oscillator is being used as a modulation source. VCO 2's waveform and pulse width controls are the same as for VCO 1.

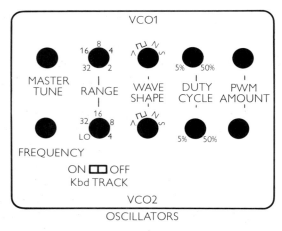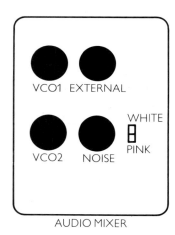

FIGURE 24: TYPICAL OSCILLATOR/MIXER BANK.

To the right of the oscillators are the level controls that make up the audio mixer. There are separate rotary controls for VCO 1, VCO 2, an external source, and for the noise source. Alongside this control is a two-position switch that selects either pink or white noise.

This is just an example of a typical oscillator and signal generator control bank. Every instrument has different configurations and facilities, but all are based on essentially the same theory. More examples of actual signal generator controls are given in Chapter 3, where several production instruments are analyzed.

THE FILTER

The filter is a glorified tone control – that's its job, to determine the timbre or tone colour of the final sound. The treble and bass controls of your record player are simple filters; however, when dealing with the synthesizer, there is a good deal more to take into consideration.

Before we look at the voltage controlled filters normally associated with the synthesizer voice module, we will firstly look at the four main types of filter and the theory involved.

An electronic filter does the same job as any other type of filter: it removes part of the material being passed through it. A tea strainer is an example of a filter: it holds back the tea leaves, letting the liquid through. Similarly, a fisherman's trawl net will let fish up to a certain size slip through, but catch the larger fish. The types of filters that are used in electronic music synthesis remove certain frequencies from the signals fed through them, and it is the filtrate, or remaining signal, which is subsequently used by the next stage of the voice module.

There are four main types of filter to contend with:

1) The low pass filter: this will remove all frequencies above a certain frequency, hence it lets low frequencies pass.

2) The high pass filter: this will remove those frequencies below a certain point.

3) The band pass filter: this will only let those parts of the signal that are of a certain frequency through.

4) The notch or band reject filter: this will remove from the signal frequencies of a certain value.

Figure 25 illustrates these filters diagrammatically. The vertical axis represents the amplitude of the frequencies which are positioned along the horizontal axis, with the higher frequencies towards the right.

If we look at the low pass filter, we can see that the graph is flat up to a certain point, then starts to trail off until the amplitude reaches zero. The point at which the amplitude starts to decrease is known as the cut-off frequency, and the rate at which the frequencies are attenuated at that point is known as the roll-off. A perfect, ideal filter wouldn't have this slope; it would be a sharp, vertical line so that all frequencies above the cut-off frequency would be completely removed – not a trace. However, this is virtually impossible, and, anyway, a filter of this type would not be a great deal of use in a conventional subtractive synthesizer – it wouldn't sound right. We'll look more closely at the cut-off frequency and the roll-on characteristic shortly.

In **figure 25,** it can be seen that the high pass filter works in much the same way as the low pass, only it is letting all the frequencies above the cut-off point pass, and attenuating those that are lower. The band pass filter allows the frequencies around the cut-off point to pass, attenuating those either side of this frequency. And the notch or band reject acts the other way round, removing only those parts of the signal that are around the cut-off point. The symbols to the right of each diagram show the short-hand representation of each of the filter configurations. These are very straightforward to understand, with the parts of the signal that that type of filter would remove being crossed out (the low pass filter

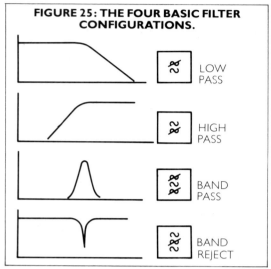

FIGURE 25: THE FOUR BASIC FILTER CONFIGURATIONS.

LOW PASS

HIGH PASS

BAND PASS

BAND REJECT

shows two sine waves with the higher one – on top – crossed out). Now, can you see how it is possible to "make" a band pass filter, using a low pass and a high pass filter with the same cut-off frequency? **Figure 26** shows how it's done. The two are arranged in series (one after another); the low pass filter will remove most of the high frequencies above the cut-off point; this signal is then fed through the high pass filter, which removes most of the low frequencies below the cut-off point. Those parts of the signal with the same frequency as the cut-off point will be almost unaffected by either filter, and will "get through." There will also be some frequencies either side of the cut-off point that will make up the final signal. However, these frequencies will have been attenuated. If you do not understand the above exercise, do go back and re-read it, as it is necessary to grasp what is happening.

Let's look again at our low pass filter, and, more particularly, at the point at which the cut-off frequency is set. **Figure 27** shows clearly that the signal starts to be attenuated actually before the point we call the cut-off frequency (fc). It isn't the case that the frequencies start to be attenuated instantaneously above the cut-off point: there is a point of adjustment such that the flat low pass area curves into the attenuation rate, or roll-off, portion. If we continue the flat line and the roll-off section, the point at which the two meet corresponds to the cut-off frequency. In actual fact, the amplitude of a sine wave at this filter will be already attenuated by 3 dB (this attenuation would be just perceptible to the human ear, if compared with a similar sine wave 3 dB louder).

The roll-off portion of the curve determines at what rate the signals are attenuated. The amplitude axis is scaled in dB's (decibels),

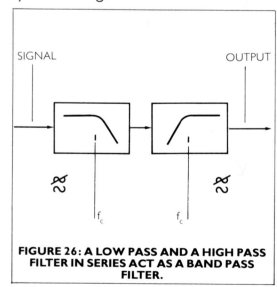

SIGNAL   OUTPUT

f_c f_c

FIGURE 26: A LOW PASS AND A HIGH PASS FILTER IN SERIES ACT AS A BAND PASS FILTER.

which is a ratio to a reference level. In this case, we are defining the flat plateau of the low pass filter as the reference point because, over this portion, the frequencies of the signal remain unaffected by the action of the filter, so, as the signal is attenuated at a certain frequency, it is considered to be –10 dB (say) in relation to the original signal. It is also necessary now to consider the horizontal frequency scale to be measured in octaves. We can now see that the low pass filter shown attenuates the signal by 6 dB for every octave that the frequency increases, so the roll-off characteristic of this filter would be said to be –6 dB/octave. Remember that the ear can only detect a difference in amplitude of 3 dB, so this rate of attenuation isn't particularly severe. It is worth noting that the amplitude of a signal halves for every 6 dB attenuation

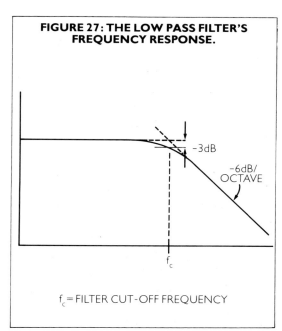

FIGURE 27: THE LOW PASS FILTER'S FREQUENCY RESPONSE.

–3dB

–6dB/ OCTAVE

f_c

f_c = FILTER CUT-OFF FREQUENCY

it undergoes; therefore, in our example **(figure 27),** if the cut-off frequency was 200 Hz, say, a sine wave of 400 Hz would be 6 dB quieter than one at the cut-off frequency and, consequently, its amplitude would be halved.

The filters used in the electronic music synthesizers are primarily voltage controlled, with the control voltage determining the cut-off frequency. These filters generally have a 6, 12, or 24 dB/octave roll-off characteristic. It is no coincidence that these are all multiples of 6: the way these filters are designed dictates that they have such a specification. These –6, –12, and –24 dB/octave filters are often referred to as 1-, 2-, and 4- pole filters respectively.

The low pass voltage controlled filter is the one to be found in all synthesizer voice modules, although many instruments employ what is known as a state variable filter. This is a circuit that will act as any of the four types of filter, so a voice module equipped with such a filter is considerably more versatile. That being said, most performers find themselves using a low pass filter for over 90% of the time.

FILTER RESONANCE

In Chapter 1, we mentioned the concept of resonance with respect to the natural harmonic series. We must now consider the way in which the filter's characteristic effect on a signal can be modified by introducing the idea of filter resonance. When dealing with a voltage controlled filter, there is normally a control associated with it that will determine the resonance. Resonance (sometimes referred to as "Q", or Emphasis) is basically a controlled feedback effect. The best way to illustrate this parameter is to look at what happens when an acoustic guitarist is playing on a stage, using a microphone and amplifier **(figure 28).** The guitarist sits down with his guitar in front of the microphone whence the sound is picked up and fed to the amplifier and speaker. Some of the sound that then comes from the speaker finds its way back to the guitar's body and to the microphone, so the microphone is now picking up both the altered sound coming from the guitar, and some part of the signal direct from the speaker. Remember how a hollow object, such as the body of a guitar, has a resonant frequency – the frequency at which the air particles prefer to vibrate. Well, if that note is played on the guitar, then the sound will have a sustaining ringing to it because the loudspeaker will act so as to perpetuate the vibration. The greater the amplification level, or the nearer the guitar is to the loudspeaker, then the greater will be this resonating feedback effect. There will come a point at which the amplification level is so great that the guitar will feed back without a note having to be played. Feedback is generally a problem when considering amplifying acoustic instruments at high levels.

If we now translate this phenomenon to our voltage controlled filter, the principle is very similar. **Figure 28** illustrates how a certain amount of the filtered signal (determined by the resonance control) is tapped off and mixed together with the incoming signal. In the zero position, the resonance control will prevent any signal being fed back to the input; however, as the control is advanced, the signal will start to "ring" until a point is reached where the filter breaks into oscillation. Surprisingly enough, this is a very desirable feature because the waveform produced at this stage is a perfect sine wave with frequency that of the cut-off point. Thus, the filter can be used as a signal generator, as well as a signal modifier.

If we now look at the diagrammatic representation of the effect of resonance **(figure 29),** we can see that the filter is, in fact, amplifying the signal around the cut-off frequency. As the resonance is increased so that the filter breaks into oscillation, the gain in amplitude around the cut-off frequency becomes of infinite value. Increasing the resonance can be seen to cause the low pass filter to start responding like a band pass filter.

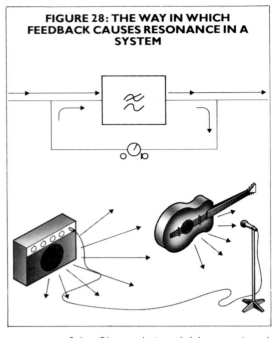

FIGURE 28: THE WAY IN WHICH FEEDBACK CAUSES RESONANCE IN A SYSTEM

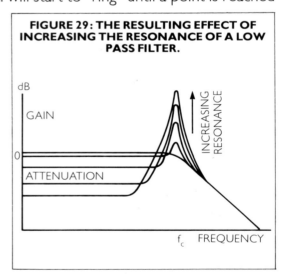

FIGURE 29: THE RESULTING EFFECT OF INCREASING THE RESONANCE OF A LOW PASS FILTER.

THE EFFECT OF THE FILTER

We have examined the theory concerning the filter cut-off frequency and the resonance; now let's look at the physical effect a filter has on a square wave. In Chapter 1, we looked at the

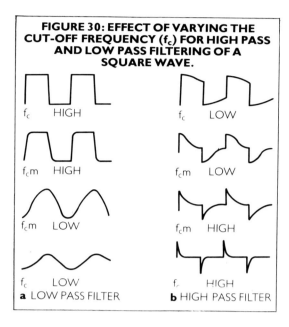

FIGURE 30: EFFECT OF VARYING THE CUT-OFF FREQUENCY (f$_c$) FOR HIGH PASS AND LOW PASS FILTERING OF A SQUARE WAVE.

f$_c$ HIGH   f$_c$ LOW

f$_c$m   HIGH   f$_c$m   LOW

f$_c$m   LOW   f$_c$m   HIGH

f$_c$ LOW   f$_c$ HIGH

a LOW PASS FILTER   **b** HIGH PASS FILTER

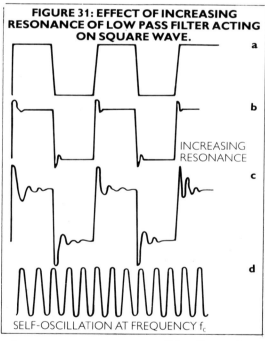

FIGURE 31: EFFECT OF INCREASING RESONANCE OF LOW PASS FILTER ACTING ON SQUARE WAVE.

a

b

INCREASING RESONANCE

c

d

SELF-OSCILLATION AT FREQUENCY f$_c$

harmonic content of the square wave and saw that it consisted of odd harmonics. **Figure 30 a** details how the filter removes the harmonics, so we can see clearly that the filter is the key to subtractive synthesis: it removes the harmonics, whilst, in additive synthesis, the sine waves are added together to produce the final tone. Note that, as the cut off frequency to the filter is reduced, the edges of the square wave become more and more rounded.

The resonance control's effect on the square wave **(figure 31)** is quite strange to see: as the resonance is increased, the square wave tends to shoot past the corner in a way similar to how a ruler, when twanged over the edge of the table, behaves. When the ruler is released, it doesn't spring back to its original position – it shoots past, then back again until the oscillations die away and it comes to rest in its initial position. The effect of increasing the resonance control causes a similar reaction – as the resonance control is increased, it takes longer for the overshoots to settle down in between changes of state (highs to lows, or vice versa). There comes the point when the filter breaks into oscillation due to the amount of feedback; then the presence of the incoming signal makes no difference to the filter's output (which is then a sine wave pitched at the cut-off frequency of the filter).

The physical effect on the sound is hard to describe verbally; however, in the case of the filtered sine wave, as the cut-off frequency is turned down through the audio spectrum, it is possible to hear the individual harmonics of the signal being removed. This is even more apparent if the resonance control is increased and the filter starts behaving like a band pass, whence any component of the filtered signal with the same (or similar) frequency to the cut-off point will be amplified, and even more easily detected by the ear **(figure 31).**

KEYBOARD TRACKING

In the diagram showing a typical synthesizer voice module block, a control voltage feed from the controller to the voltage controlled filter is drawn in. This is a very important feature, and one that some manufacturers fail to consider in their instruments. Take, for example, a sawtooth wave, which is pitched at 100 Hz when the bottom note of the keyboard (controller) is played, and at 1600 Hz when the top note is played (that's four octaves range). If the low pass filter cut-off frequency is set to 400 Hz, say, then, over the bottom two octaves, the fundamental component of the sawtooth wave will be unaffected, whereas, as the waveform is pitched higher up the keyboard, the filter's effect will be increasingly apparent. The resulting sound will be as if the note was being muffled, the higher its pitch. This isn't generally a good state of affairs, and it is for this reason that a facility whereby the filter tracks the pitch of the oscillator's is included in most synthesizer voice modules. There are occasions when 1:1 tracking, i.e. for every octave rise in the oscillators pitch, the filter cut-off frequency increases by one octave, isn't required, and many instruments offer some form of proportional tracking control.

In the last section, dealing with resonance, we mentioned that, if the resonance control is advanced too far, the filter breaks into oscillation at a frequency of that of the cut-off point. If there is a keyboard (or controller) track facility, it then becomes possible to "play" the filter, just as if it were a voltage controlled oscillator. The waveform produced is a pure sine wave, so no further form of filtering would make any difference. This arrangement is particularly suitable for producing flute-like simulations.

It may seem strange to many people, but filters vary from manufacturer to manufacturer. Unlike an oscillator, where a sawtooth wave produced by an instrument's oscillator will sound the same as that produced by any other, filters behave in a different manner. Obviously, one −24 dB/octave filter (say), if it conforms perfectly to its amplitude/frequency response curve, will behave like any other such filter. However, it is possible to introduce elements of signal distortion (bass boost, etc.) in order to give a filter a certain characteristic sound. Therefore, one make of synthesizer, although it may have essentially the same features as a competitor, can sound quite different, and this is completely due to the type of filter.

The filter is like the body of a violin: it imparts its own specific tonal characteristics on the sound produced. It is sometimes possible, with experience, to identify, from a piece of music, the make of synthesizer being used, and this is purely as a result of the response of the filter.

Many synthesizers employ filters that offer a choice of roll-off – i.e. 2-pole (12 dB/octave) or 4-pole (24 dB/octave). This is a handy facility, as, in some circumstances, a 2-pole filter is better suited to the task (and vice versa). This use of the filter is discussed further in Chapter 4.

Up until recently, there was a distinct difference in the quality of sound of Eastern and Western filters. The Japanese tended to build instruments that had a much thinner, almost nasal, quality to them, whilst the American and European manufacturers generally went for a fuller, richer sound. The West seems to have won this battle, primarily as a result of the synthesizer being predominantly used in rock (and associated) areas of music. More recently, the Japanese have been producing instruments with a more "Western" sound.

The timbre of a note produced by an acoustic instrument varies over its duration, so a synthesizer must be able to do likewise. Therefore, it is necessary to have some way of changing the cut-off frequency of the filter as the note is sounding. The way in which this is achieved is discussed under APERIODIC VARIATIONS OF TIMBRE WITH TIME.

THE AMPLIFIER

This part of the synthesizer voice module is essentially the simplest to understand. Again, this device is voltage controlled and behaves such that it amplifies or attenuates a signal in amount proportional to the voltage applied to it. It is used almost exclusively in conjunction with an envelope generator, in order to give a note dynamics – i.e. to shape the contours of the sound. See APERIODIC VARIATIONS OF LOUDNESS WITH TIME.

THE ENVELOPE GENERATOR

This device produces no actual sound itself, but merely a control voltage which is used to modulate any of the voltage controllable parameters. Every sound has an envelope – a start, a middle and an end – and the voltage produced by the envelope generator traces out a contour that can be used to shape the amplitude and timbre of sound. It can also be used to sweep the pitch of the note.

There are several variations on the types of envelope generator but, essentially, they all stem from the ADSR envelope **(figure 32).** The contour of a note is, in the case of the ADSR envelope, defined by the four distinct parameters:

1 – The **A**ttack time: the period the contour takes to reach its maximum voltage amplitude after a trigger or gate pulse has been received by the envelope generator;

2 – The **D**ecay time: the period that it takes for the contour to fall from the maximum level to . . . .

3 – The **S**ustain level: the voltage to which the contour decays, assuming that the envelope generator is still receiving a gate pulse (i.e. the note is still being held);

4 – The **R**elease time: the period that it takes for the contour to fall away from the release level to the initial voltage level after the gate pulse has disappeared (i.e. the note has been released).

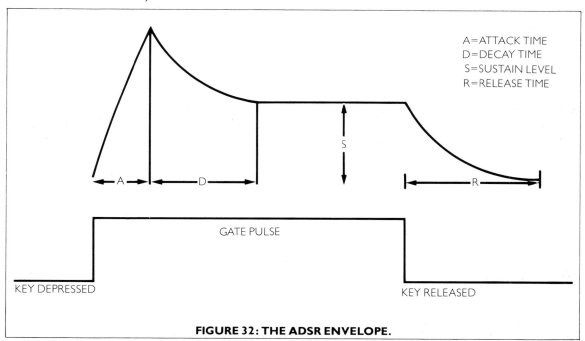

FIGURE 32: THE ADSR ENVELOPE.

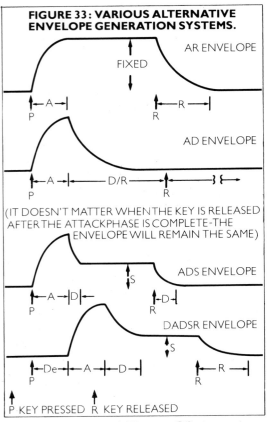

FIGURE 33: VARIOUS ALTERNATIVE ENVELOPE GENERATION SYSTEMS.

AR ENVELOPE

FIXED

AD ENVELOPE

(IT DOESN'T MATTER WHEN THE KEY IS RELEASED AFTER THE ATTACK PHASE IS COMPLETE - THE ENVELOPE WILL REMAIN THE SAME)

ADS ENVELOPE

DADSR ENVELOPE

P KEY PRESSED   R KEY RELEASED

Some of these terms are often found confusing, especially "Decay," "Sustain," and "Release". In synthesizer terminology, the phrase "increasing the attack (time) of a note" can also be confusing. In respect of the envelope generator, this means that the attack time should be given a higher value; consequently, the note would take longer to reach its maximum amplitude.

Commonly found variants of the ADSR envelope generator are: the AR (attack release) envelope which produces a voltage that rises to a maximum level (A), where it remains until the note is released (R), the AD envelope – the note rises to a maximum (A), then instantaneously decays (D) to the initial voltage; the ADS envelope – which rises to a maximum (A), then decays (D) to the sustain level (S), where it continues until the gate is released whence it falls to the initial position again at the decay rate (D). Some envelope generators also have an additional "Delay" parameter, whereby the attack of the note doesn't start to happen until a certain set period of time after the envelope generator has been triggered. **Figure 33** shows how most of these "spin-off" envelopes can be treated from an ADSR envelope. Study this table and make sure that you understand the reasonings behind how the ADSR envelope can be used to generate the other types. So, for the ADSR simulation of an AD envelope, why should the R(elease) time be set to the same value as the D(ecay)? Well, if the ADSR envelope were to receive a gate pulse with duration less than

Attack/Release envelope is equivalent to	Attack – **Variable** Decay – **Setting doesn't matter** Sustain – **Maximum** Release – **Variable**	
Attack/Decay envelope is equivalent to	Attack – **Variable** Decay – **Variable** Sustain – **Zero** Release – **Equal to decay time**	
Attack/Decay/Sustain envelope is equivalent to	Attack – **Variable** Decay – **Variable** Sustain – **Variable** Release – **Equal to decay time**	

FIGURE 34: HOW VARIOUS ENVELOPES CAN BE SIMULATED USING AN ADSR ENVELOPE.

that of the envelope, then, as the key was released, the decay would become the release, and, unless the two settings correspond, the shape of the envelope would be upset. This is just a technical exercise to get you familiar with the workings of the envelope generator; in Chapter 4, the way in which the ADSR envelope can be used to simulate the contours of existing instruments is examined.

Before moving on to that, there are a couple of other envelope features that may sometimes be encountered. First, there is "proportional tracking" of the control voltage, used to determine the pitch of the note (i.e. from the controller) by the envelope generator. This is a relatively new development, and is only just starting to appear on some makes of synthesizer. It is based on the theory that the envelope of some acoustic instruments (both loudness and timbral) changes with the pitch of the note played. For example, a bowed instrument, such as a 'cello, responds faster the higher the note being played. So, in order to translate this principle of "acoustic inertia" to the synthesizer, in some models the control voltage is fed to the envelope generator, and the attack, decay, and release parameters can be shortened as the control voltage increases.

The second feature, not so relevant to the simulation of existing instruments, is the envelope cycle, or repeat function. This behaves such that, when the envelope finally returns to its initial position, i.e. as the release time expires, then a pulse is generated which causes the envelope to fire again, so it's back to the attack period, and so on. The envelope generator is now cycling round, independent of the controller's trigger pulse. The envelope waveform can really no longer be considered aperiodic – it is repeating itself in a definite pattern and is therefore a periodic vibration. If, say, the release time is decreased whilst the envelope is cycling round, then the duration of the entire cycle is decreased, and so the frequency is increased. This repeat mode function is a different concept to using a low frequency pulse instead of the one from the controller (keyboard) to activate the envelope. See PERIODIC VARIATIONS OF AMPLITUDE WITH TIME.

A typical envelope generator would look something like **figure 35.** Many manufacturers seem to prefer the use of sliders as opposed to control knobs for the envelope controls – they do give a more graphic representation of the shape of the envelope.

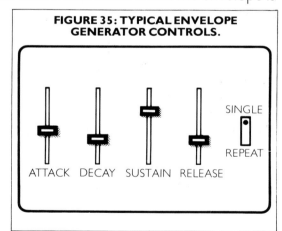

FIGURE 35: TYPICAL ENVELOPE GENERATOR CONTROLS.

ATTACK   DECAY   SUSTAIN   RELEASE   SINGLE   REPEAT

THE LOW FREQUENCY OSCILLATOR (LFO)

We touched briefly on this matter when discussing the voltage controlled oscillator. However, nearly all synthesizer voice modules incorporate a non-voltage controlled low frequency oscillator which produces a periodic sub-audio control waveform for modulating any voltage controllable parameter. Most LFO's cover the range between 0.2 Hz (one oscillation every five seconds) up to 35 Hz, or thereabouts. It can be quite useful, as we shall see later, to have a modulation frequency well up into the audio band: that's why many dual oscillator synthesizer voice modules can be set such that the second VCO acts as a modulation oscillator. As the LFO isn't voltage controllable, the rate of oscillation is set by a simple control knob; and, for any given sound, that rate is normally left constant.

A low frequency oscillator must provide sine (though triangle is usually acceptable) and square waveforms; it is also useful to have a sawtooth waveform (ramp up and ramp down) and a random, or sample-and-hold, waveshape. We have already discussed most of these waveforms, on oscillators, and the way in which they are used is covered in the next couple of sections. However, we haven't dealt with the random signal.

RANDOM, OR SAMPLE-AND-HOLD WAVEFORMS

A random modulation waveform can almost be considered to be a sub-audio noise source, but it isn't quite so straightforward. **Figure 36** shows how this waveform is produced. It is necessary to start with a source waveform: this is usually the white noise generator, but it doesn't have to be. This waveform is then "sampled", i.e. it is looked at for a fraction of a second, and, at that instant, the voltage of the source waveform is fed to a hold circuit which sits at that level until it receives another sample pulse whence it holds the source waveform's new voltage level **(figure 37).** The rate at which the source waveform is sampled is determined by the frequency control of the LFO, so the resulting signal is changing at regular intervals, but to random voltages.

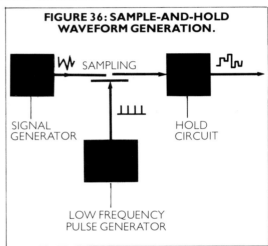

FIGURE 36: SAMPLE-AND-HOLD WAVEFORM GENERATION.

SAMPLING

SIGNAL GENERATOR

HOLD CIRCUIT

LOW FREQUENCY PULSE GENERATOR

PERIODIC VARIATION OF PITCH WITH TIME (LFO + VCO)

The low frequency oscillator generates a periodic (repeating) voltage, which can be used to modulate any voltage controllable parameter. When used in conjunction with the VCO's, the LFO is said to be frequency modulating the pitch. The most common form of frequency modulation must be vibrato. This occurs when a sine wave causes the frequency of a note to increase and decrease smoothly. Because it is more expensive for synthesizer manufacturers to construct low frequency oscillators that generate sine rather than triangle waves, you will find that a lot of instruments incorporate the latter. In fact, for most purposes, this is sufficient. **Figure 38** shows exactly what is happening to a frequency modulated sine wave.

The other common form of frequency modulation of the oscillators is "trill", and again, this is simply accomplished by using a low frequency square wave as the modulating source **figure 39.** As a square wave exists in two states (high and low), the frequency of the VCO will, therefore, oscillate between two notes, their relative pitches being determined by the amplitude of the square wave signal.

The most important aspect regarding any form of modulation is the way in which it is introduced. Consider a violinist and the way in which he uses frequency modulation to add both depth and expression to the notes he is playing. He tends to introduce modulation towards the end of a note or phrase. A synthesizer can be used in an identical manner, with the modulation introduced as and when necessary, either automatically, using the LFO delay function, or, better still, manually, using a performance control. This is usually a device much like a control knob, conveniently positioned or incorporated in the controller, in order that certain parameters of the overall sound can be quickly and easily changed. See Chapter 2.

Sawtooth frequency modulation is generally limited to special effects, such as sirens, and hooters (ramp up). Similarly, random frequency modulation is seldom used except for bizarre, spacey effects.

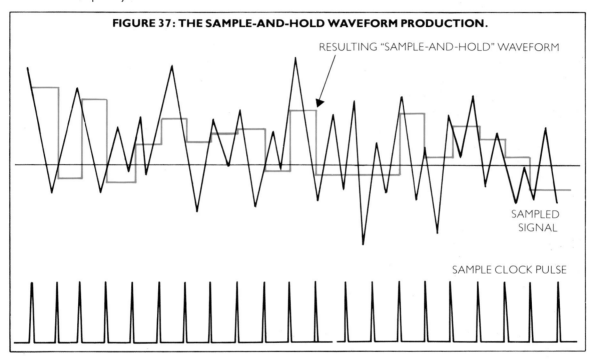

FIGURE 37: THE SAMPLE-AND-HOLD WAVEFORM PRODUCTION.

RESULTING "SAMPLE-AND-HOLD" WAVEFORM

SAMPLED SIGNAL

SAMPLE CLOCK PULSE

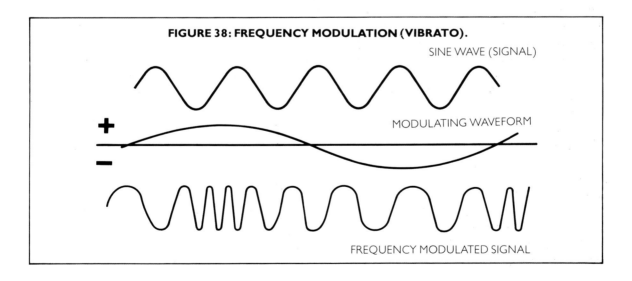

FIGURE 38: FREQUENCY MODULATION (VIBRATO).

SINE WAVE (SIGNAL)

MODULATING WAVEFORM

FREQUENCY MODULATED SIGNAL

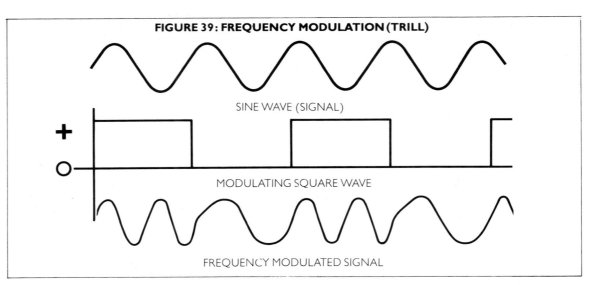

FIGURE 39: FREQUENCY MODULATION (TRILL)

SINE WAVE (SIGNAL)

MODULATING SQUARE WAVE

FREQUENCY MODULATED SIGNAL

PERIODIC VARIATION OF TIMBRE WITH TIME (LFO + VCF)

The low frequency oscillator can also be used to vary the cut-off frequency of the filter, and is known as wow-wow, wah-wah, or some similar onomatopoeic name. Musically, the effect is rather limited; however, it can be used in conjunction with VCO modulation, so, as the pitch of the note increases, the filter cut-off frequency follows suit accordingly. It's a similar principle to that of the filter tracking the keyboard.

When using a low frequency oscillator to modulate the filter, the setting of the cut-off frequency control has a lot to do with the effect produced. The waveform produced by the LFO is centred around the zero volt position, so, if we were using a sine wave, say, during the positive part of the cycle, the cut-off frequency would be increased, whilst, during the negative stage, the frequency is lowered. If, therefore, the filter was set fully open, i.e. the cut-off frequency (if it were a low pass filter) was having little effect on even the highest audible components of the signal, then the positive portion of the cycle would have no effect on the resultant sound. The cut-off frequency needs, therefore, to be adjusted so that the cycle does have the desired effect on the final sound.

Various interesting sounds can be obtained by using a high frequency modulation wave-form to modulate the filter cut-off frequency. This can be all the more striking if the filter resonance is increased to the point that it almost breaks into oscillation. A considerable number of overtones are set up, and the sound produced can be used as a basis for simulating, for example, a human voice.

The random pattern of the LFO is put to best use when frequency modulating the filter: again, the filter should be set with a fair amount of resonance, and, if the cut-off frequency is set to the right position, a striking rhythmic pattern will be generated.

PERIODIC VARIATION OF LOUDNESS WITH TIME (LFO + VCA)

The low frequency oscillator's third possible area of influence is to vary the loudness of the note – amplitude modulation. **Figure 40** illustrates a low frequency sine wave being used as an amplitude modulator. It can clearly be seen that the shape of this waveform is defined by the modulated signal and a configuration of this nature is more commonly known as tremolo.

If a square wave is used as the modulating source, the signal's amplitude will switch between two stages, and, in extreme cases (i.e. when a square wave with a large amplitude itself is used in this fashion), the low position of the cycle will cause the voltage controlled amplifier to attenuate the signal, so that it is effectively inaudible.

Obviously, the other LFO waveforms could be used to vary the loudness; however, their usage is less common.

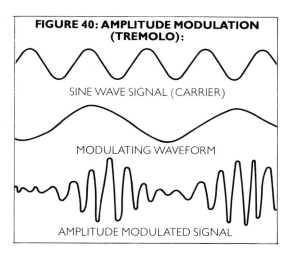

FIGURE 40: AMPLITUDE MODULATION (TREMOLO):

SINE WAVE SIGNAL (CARRIER)

MODULATING WAVEFORM

AMPLITUDE MODULATED SIGNAL

APERIODIC VARIATION OF PITCH WITH TIME
(ENVELOPE GENERATOR + VCO)

As we've already learnt, an aperiodic waveform is one that has no recognizable pattern – it does not repeat itself. The sources of aperiodic waveforms in a synthesizer voice module are the envelope generators, and the white/pink noise generator. Although many synthesizers provide facilities for modulating the pitch of the note by a noise source, the use of such a configuration is fairly limited: it is primarily used for special effects. Modulation of the pitch of the note with an envelope control voltage can often be put to a more "musical" application. It is vital, when working with such a set-up, to be able to set the amount of envelope generator voltage used to "sweep" the pitch of the note. Normally, only a very small amount of modulation is used. However, one very important aspect of aperiodic pitch modulation is wrapped up in the subject of "oscillator synchronization", which is dealt with fully – later in this chapter.

APERIODIC VARIATION OF TIMBRE WITH TIME
(ENVELOPE GENERATOR + VCF)

We have already mentioned that, for all acoustic instruments, the harmonic content of a note varies over its duration. It is this fact that makes synthesis of such instruments as a piano so difficult. The way in which the subtractive synthesizer attempts to simulate this control change harmonic structure is by using an envelope generator to vary the cut-off frequency of the filter. This isn't a perfect solution: ideally, it would be necessary to have a complex envelope generator capable of producing an envelope of any shape, for every harmonic note – which is, in essence, the way in which an additive synthesizer functions. However, the ADSR (or similar) filter envelope generator is remarkably useful, and there are few occasions when a close approximation of the desired effect isn't possible.

A synthesizer voice module really does need to have two separate envelope generators – one for the VCA and one for the VCF. Some of the cheaper instruments try to cut corners by using the same envelope for both purposes: the lack of performance this causes is obviously reflected in the lower price of the instrument, but, with only one envelope, an entire area of the synthesis process becomes virtually unavailable to the player.

The sound produced by aperiodically modulating the filter is probably what the synthesizer has become best known for; when used with the normal low pass filter, the characteristic "Beeooww" of the filter cut-off frequency sweeping down can be heard. The two controls that primarily determine the resulting character of the sound are the cut-off frequency control of the filter, and the envelope amount control. **Figure 41** shows how these two parameters combine together to shape the timbre. This time, the vertical axis of the diagram represents the combined voltage from the envelope generator and the cut-off control knob, which corresponds to the resulting changes in cut-off frequency of the filter being used on the incoming signal. It is clear that the filter amount control determines the depth of the "Beeooww", whilst the cut-off frequency control knob sets the frequency around which the envelope operates. This is sometimes known as the filter bias voltage (or frequency).

Let's look in detail at what is happening in a more specific case. Say that the signal to be filtered by a 12 dB/octave low pass filter is a sawtooth wave, oscillating at 220 Hz. So, **figure 42** shows the harmonic structure of the source up to the fifth harmonic: the first harmonic (the fundamental) is considered to be the reference 0dB, so the second harmonic

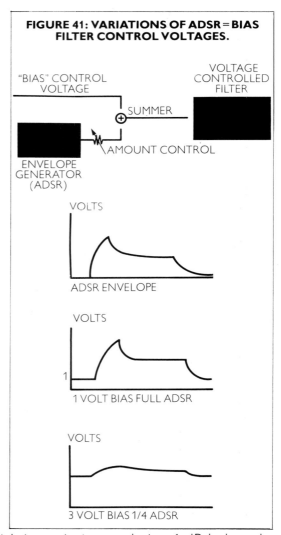

FIGURE 41: VARIATIONS OF ADSR = BIAS FILTER CONTROL VOLTAGES.

will be at 440 Hz and half the amplitude, which is equivalent to being 6 dB below the fundamental. Similarly, the third harmonic is at 660 Hz (220 × 3), and one-third the amplitude of the fundamental (–9.54 dB). There are, of course, further harmonics present. However, in order to keep this example relatively simple, we will ignore those above the fifth. The envelope with which we are going to modulate the filter we'll take to be an AD type: fast attack, slow decay. First, let's set the filter (bias) cut-off frequency, so that the filter is running at 220 Hz. So, in **figure 42(b),** we can see that the fundamental has been attenuated 3 dB (remember that the cut-off frequency point is always –3 dB against the flat portion); then the filter removes the higher harmonics at a rate of 12 dB/octave, so the second harmonic will be 18 dB (–12–6) below the fundamental. Similarly, the fourth harmonic will be –24 dB with respect to the fundamental (the fourth harmonic is initially 12 dB below the fundamental, but, as it is two octaves above the cut-off frequency, it is also undergoing a further 24 dB attenuation). Now, 36 dB is quite a considerable reduction in the amplitude of the note – in fact, the amplitude is one sixty-fourth that of the fundamental.

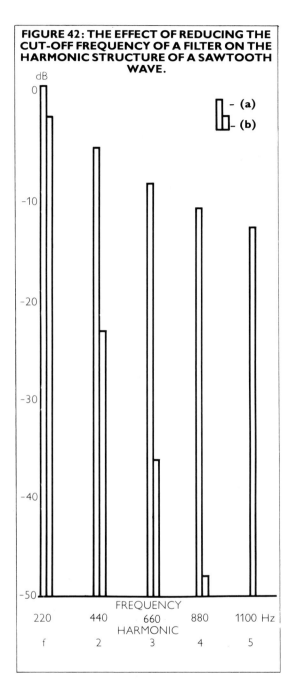

FIGURE 42: THE EFFECT OF REDUCING THE CUT-OFF FREQUENCY OF A FILTER ON THE HARMONIC STRUCTURE OF A SAWTOOTH WAVE.

If we now introduce a voltage from the envelope generator of, say, two volts peak (at the height of the attack phase), what will happen is that the filter cut-off frequency, because it responds to control voltages with a one volt/octave ratio, will open out to 880 Hz at the height of the envelope; that means that the fourth harmonic, instead of being attenuated 24 dB by the filter, is now only 3 dB down because of the effect of the filter. As the envelope decays away, however, the cut-off frequency starts to fall, and the higher harmonics start to disappear.

If, instead of biasing the filter cut-off point at 220 Hz, we set it right down at 55 Hz, then the effect of the envelope generator would be far more dramatic. Initially, with the filter set at this point, all the harmonics would be 24 dB less than for the above example. At its maximum point, (i.e. at the peak of the envelope), the position would be as in **figure 42a** and, as the envelope dies away, most of the harmonics would be severely attenuated. Thus, it can be seen that, not only does the envelope generator affect the *timbre* of the filtrate, but also the *amplitude,* and, when the cut-off frequency is biased at a particularly low level, the voltage controlled filter can be used as a kind of voltage controlled amplifier.

In our above example, it is fairly obvious that the greater the amount of the envelope voltage allowed to control the filter, then proportionally more higher harmonics of the signal will be present. But it can also be seen that, if the filter is biased much above the fundamental of the signal, then the filter has little scope to operate from, as it can only remove the frequencies above the cut-off point.

APERIODIC VARIATION OF AMPLITUDE WITH TIME (ENVELOPE GENERATOR + VCF)

The amplitude of a note has to vary with time, otherwise that sound will drone on *ad infinitum*. In order to "shape" a sound, an envelope generator is used in conjunction with a voltage controlled amplifier. **Figure 43** shows the output voltage of a typical envelope generator being fed into a VCA in order to shape an incoming signal – in this case, a sine wave. The resulting waveform can be seen to contain the basic sine wave signal, but with the amplitude shaped to the envelope. Note that this resulting signal is mirrored about the centre line. If you think about it, this has to be the case: if the incoming waveform is attenuated/amplified by the same amount in both the positive and negative phases of the cycle, a waveform such as shown in **figure 43 (b)** just wouldn't happen. For a start, those sharp corners would completely change the character of the sound.

Let's now look at the ADSR (attack, decay, sustain, release) envelope and see how the various parameters operate in conjunction with the voltage controlled amplifier. The attack phase is probably the most important part of a note. The brain is at maximum concentration when a new note is played, and, from the information presented in the first fraction of a second, it knows more or less what to expect from the body of the note. The phenomena is rather like that experienced when we talk (or, in fact, read): we detect the first part of a word and our brains, generally, can work out what is going to happen next. It is for this reason that the attack phase of a note is so important. The amplitude envelope of, say, a flute, or trumpet, is fairly fast and these instruments are said to have little acoustic inertia. But, a violin, or other similar instrument, has to have a bow accelerated across its strings, so the attack time will be somewhat slower. All percussive instruments – those where a medium is being struck (a piano has hammers that strike the strings, a vibraphone is played using hammers to strike tuned bars), – have an almost instantaneous attack characteristic. Similarly, plucked instruments, such as the harpsichord or classical guitar, also have an almost instantaneous attack portion of the loudness envelope.

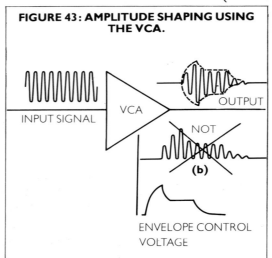

FIGURE 43: AMPLITUDE SHAPING USING THE VCA.

INPUT SIGNAL
VCA
OUTPUT
NOT
(b)
ENVELOPE CONTROL VOLTAGE

The decay phase is generally used to identify the percussive and plucked voices. The sounds produced by harpsichords and pianos will always eventually die away, no matter how long the note is held. The decay of the amplitude envelope is, therefore, closely related to the third portion of the envelope: the sustain level. A plucked or percussive instrument will not have any sustain level, as the sound will always die away. A compromise is necessary when using a synthesizer, in order that the decay phase can be distinguished from the release time. Let's reconsider the amplitude envelope of an acoustic piano.

Figure 44 shows a simplified representation of such an envelope. As you can see, the attack portion is almost instantaneous; then the amplitude drops initially very quickly, but then more gradually. Finally, when the key is released, assuming that the strings are still sounding, their vibrations are damped by the felts of the piano, and the sound dies away fairly rapidly. So we've got here an attack, a decay/sustain, and a release phase of the sound. How best are we going to use the ADSR envelope to recreate *this* envelope? The

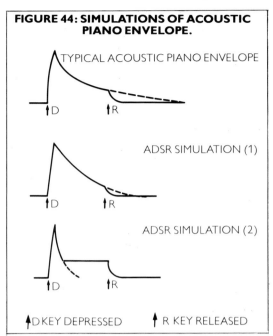

FIGURE 44: SIMULATIONS OF ACOUSTIC PIANO ENVELOPE.

TYPICAL ACOUSTIC PIANO ENVELOPE

D   R

ADSR SIMULATION (1)

D   R

ADSR SIMULATION (2)

D   R

↑D KEY DEPRESSED   ↑ R KEY RELEASED

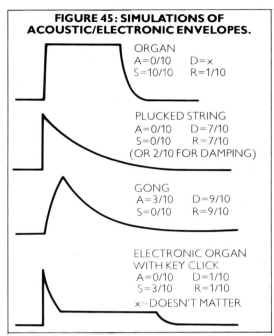

FIGURE 45: SIMULATIONS OF ACOUSTIC/ELECTRONIC ENVELOPES.

ORGAN
A=0/10   D=x
S=10/10   R=1/10

PLUCKED STRING
A=0/10   D=7/10
S=0/10   R=7/10
(OR 2/10 FOR DAMPING)

GONG
A=3/10   D=9/10
S=0/10   R=9/10

ELECTRONIC ORGAN
WITH KEY CLICK
A=0/10   D=1/10
S=3/10   R=1/10
x=DOESN'T MATTER

attack portion is straightforward enough – a very short attack time. We now have two alternatives: 1) set the sustain level to zero, so we have a relatively slow decay time and fast release, which will result in an envelope as shown in **figure 44;** or 2) set the sustain level to around one third the maximum envelope level, and have a fast decay, and fast or slow release, depending on the type of piano sound required – a long release would correspond to depressing the piano's "sustain" pedal. Notice how important the duration of the gate signal (how long the note is held) is to the shape of the envelope. In Chapter 4, we will examine further ways of influencing the shape of the envelope by the playing style.

Figure 45 illustrates other amplitude envelopes for acoustic instruments, and the way in which these can be simulated using the ADSR envelope generator.

We've now dealt with the main features of the circuit blocks that form a synthesizer voice module. There are, however, several other facilities that are often to be found as part of a voice module. These should be discussed.

SYNCHRONIZATION (VCO 1, VCO 2 AND CONTROL WAVEFORM)

The effect known as synchronization is primarily related to the voltage controlled oscillator section of a dual oscillator voice module. Having these two waveforms running almost in unison, you will remember, gave an extra depth and fullness to the sound. Strangely, the effect of synchronization acts to destroy this "free phase" quality, and causes the two oscillators to become locked together, such that all beat frequencies are eliminated. But there are other benefits to be gained from this linking of the two oscillators.

Consider a dual oscillator synthesizer voice module with, for the sake of argument, both oscillators producing sawtooth waves and being tuned almost in unison. If this module is equipped with a "sync" facility, it will manifest itself as a simple on/off switch. So, if the output is being monitored by activating the sync switch, any form of beating between the two oscillators will be instantly cancelled, and the two oscillators will sound as one.

Figure 46 shows an exaggerated representation of what is happening. Oscillator 2 can be seen to be vibrating at a faster rate than Oscillator 1, (i.e. it is slightly sharper in pitch).

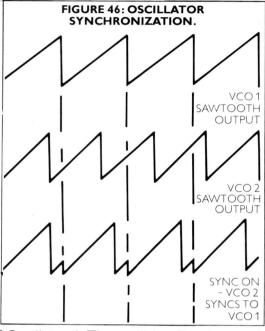

FIGURE 46: OSCILLATOR SYNCHRONIZATION.

VCO 1 SAWTOOTH OUTPUT

VCO 2 SAWTOOTH OUTPUT

SYNC ON - VCO 2 SYNCS TO VCO 1

In this example, let's say that the voice module has been designed such that Oscillator 2 will lock onto, or sync up with, Oscillator 1. (Of course, it can be the other way around, for different machines). So, when the two oscillators undergo synchronization, every time Oscillator 1 resets and starts a new cycle, it causes Oscillator 2 to do likewise – this new waveform can be seen in the diagram, and, because both oscillators are now being reset at the same time, they will be phase-related.

If the difference in frequencies between the two oscillators is increased (i.e. Oscillator 2 is sharpened), then the synchronized waveform will tend towards the second harmonic; that is to say, the second part of the cycle will become larger, and there'll come a point when Oscillator 2 is running at twice the frequency of Oscillator 1. The audible effect is a most interesting one. The synchronized waveform tends to highlight the harmonic series of the rooted oscillator (1), but, in addition, there are several other complex overtones caused by the resetting of the waveform, and, as a result, the new waveform is very rich in harmonics – and not all of them simply related.

Synchronization can be used as a static or a dynamic effect. Statically, the frequency of Oscillator 2 would be set at such a pitch as to give the desired tonal effect, which can then be further filtered by the VCF as necessary. An envelope generator, normally the one used to modulate the filter, can be employed to "bend" the pitch of the synchronized oscillator (2). This causes the harmonics of the resulting signal to be varied aperiodically with time, following the contour of the envelope generator. The effect is much like that of envelope modulation of the filter cut-off frequency, but the sound produced, because it is creating extra overtones, is much harder and somewhat metallic.

Synchronization can be a very useful tool – not so much in the simulation of existing musical instruments, but more in the creation of abstract voicings.

THE HIGH PASS FILTER (STATIC)

It is sometimes the case that a more comprehensive synthesizer voice module will be equipped with a high pass filter. This is usually positioned after the low pass voltage controlled filter, and is used to remove any unwanted low frequencies remaining after the signal has had certain high frequency components removed. This is a static filter – not voltage controlled – and generally consists of just one control which sets the cut-off frequency. Although this feature is none too common, it does have a lot of power in determining the overall timbre of the synthesizer sound.

CROSS MODULATION

Cross modulation **(figure 47)** is another effect found, for the most part, on dual oscillator synthesizers only; it is simply the use of one voltage controlled oscillator to modulate either the frequency of the other oscillator, or the cut-off frequency of the filter. Consider the former arrangement. It is often the case that this oscillator can be switched to a low frequency setting and isolated from the keyboard control voltage; in this situation, the set-up is the same as if you were using the conventional LFO arrangement. It is only by introducing the keyboard control voltage to the modulating oscillator, or by increasing its frequency into the audio spectrum, that unusual things start to happen. By introducing the control voltage to the modulating VCO, the effect should be obvious – a modulating rate dependent on the note being played. What happens when the modulating oscillator is taken up into the audio spectrum isn't quite so obvious.

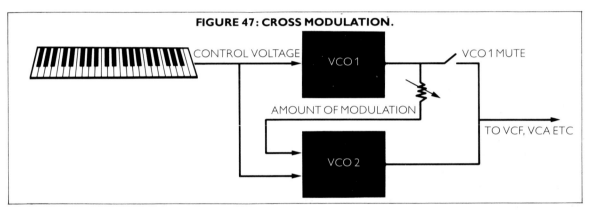

FIGURE 47: CROSS MODULATION.

CONTROL VOLTAGE

VCO 1

VCO 1 MUTE

AMOUNT OF MODULATION

TO VCF, VCA ETC

VCO 2

As the frequency of the modulating oscillator enters the region of 30 to 50 Hz, the modulated sound loses its clean, pure-pitched quality, and the sound becomes muddled and often discordant. This is due to things called sidebands, which manifest themselves as harmonics that are out of tune with the modulated oscillator. When we were dealing with more conventional sub-audio frequency modulation, these sidebands weren't perceptible, as they too were below the threshold frequency of the human ear. The sidebands cause the waveform produced to be very rich in harmonics, and, subsequently, can be used to simulate clangorous sounds (gongs, bells, and so on). As the modulating oscillator can be switched to track the keyboard, the interval between the modulating and modulated oscillators can be made to remain constant, and it is therefore possible to produce the same musical timbres across the entire keyboard. If the modulating oscillator did not track the keyboard, then the harmonics caused by the sidebands would move in opposite directions as the pitch of the modulated oscillator changed.

Cross modulation can also be used on the voltage controlled filter, with similar fascinating results. By virtue of the change in phase caused by varying the cut-off frequency of a voltage controlled filter, the pitch of any note being acted on by the filter will be altered during this transition. The theory behind this phenomenon is beyond the scope of this book, but the filter, when modulated by a sine wave, will impart a true vibrato on the source signal. The vibrato won't, however, sound the same as simply frequency modulating the VCO.

RING MODULATION

A ring modulator **(figure 48)** is a separate device distinct from the oscillators, filter, amplifier and envelope generators. Its purpose is to analyze two input signals and produce two outputs: one is a signal made up of a waveform whose frequency is the arithmetical sum of the frequencies of the two input signals; the other output is made up of a signal with frequency equivalent to the difference between the two inputs.

So, say VCO 1 is producing a signal at 220 Hz, and VCO 2 is running at 330 Hz: if these two signals were to be ring modulated together, then the resulting signals would be of 550 Hz, and 110 Hz. Again, this facility is used to produce waveforms that are rich in harmonics, which are most desirable in subtractive synthesis. If the two input signals aren't "related" to one another, (i.e. one isn't a harmonic of the other), then the ring modulator's output can be very complex indeed, especially as it is usually the case that manufacturers mix together the sum and difference output signals to make a composite output.

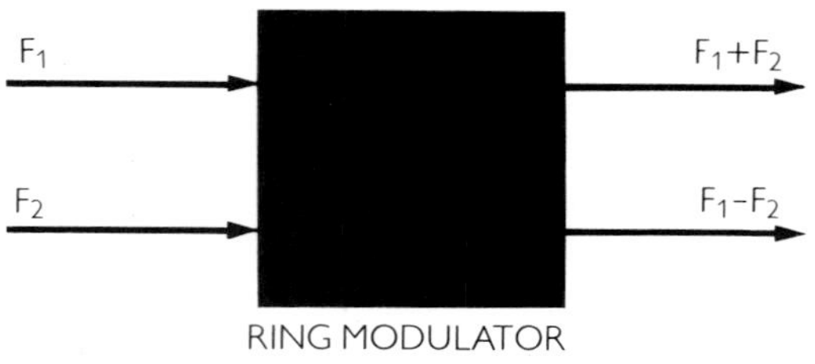

The ring modulator has a further use, which can be illustrated if we consider what happens when a signal (of, say, 220 Hz) is ring modulated with a steady d.c. voltage, which can be considered to be a signal of frequency 0 Hz. In fact, nothing would happen – the steady voltage inhibits the output of the ring modulator (due to an effect known as phase reversal – the sum and difference cancelling one another out). But, as soon as the voltage changes, then the ring modulator will jump into action, producing a signal of the sum and difference of the input frequencies. This will be rather strange because the output will be almost identical to the signal input as the voltage can be considered now to have a frequency of less than 1 Hz. The output level of the ring modulator is dependent on the rate of change of the voltage (again, due to the phase relationship); consequently, it is possible to use the ring modulator as a voltage – change controlled amplifier.

FIGURE 48: THE RING MODULATOR.

F_1 → □ → F_1+F_2

F_2 → □ → F_1-F_2

RING MODULATOR

THE KEYBOARD AND PERFORMANCE CONTROLS

Before discussing the application of the synthesizer voice module in the various types of synthesizer currently available, we should firstly look at the most common form of synthesizer controller – the keyboard. In particular, we'll look at the devices known as performance controls, as it is these that make what is essentially an electronic machine into a musical instrument.

A violinist injects expression into his playing by subtle control of timbre, volume and vibrato; a guitarist does likewise, also "bending" the strings in order to raise the pitch in a smooth manner. Well, a synthesizer is capable of having all these parameters modified during the course of a note, or run of notes; all that is required is that a certain control knob should be advanced, or retarded, as necessary.

To make matters simpler, the synthesizer designers developed performance controls which were specially designed to make it quick and easy for the player to vary certain parameters whilst he/she is actually playing the instrument. Each manufacturer adopts a different approach, devising better, more comfortable, and more controllable devices, so we will take a look at some of the most popular, and how and what they are used for.

PITCHBEND

The most frequently used performance control is the pitchbender, as it allows the player to break out of the fixed semitonal scale, and actually to "get between" the notes. The prime requirement of a good pitchbender is that it can be easily used to raise or lower the pitch of the oscillators a certain amount, but that it will also return exactly to its initial position when not in use, so that the synthesizer will remain in tune.

So, basically, what this control is doing is adding a voltage to the VCO's when the pitch is to be raised, or supplying a negative voltage when the pitch is to be lowered. When not in use, the control sits at zero volts, having no effect.

The range of the pitchbender is very important. Some instruments have a switchable range control that predetermines the effect the performance control is going to have in its maximum position. This can result in a frequency shift of a tone, a fifth, or more than an octave; other models just have a fixed range. It is vital that the performance control provides a pitchbend of at least a fifth up, and a fifth down.

MODULATION AMOUNT

The other most important performance control determines the modulation amount. This one doesn't have to return to a central position as it is just adding to the control signal. Generally, the modulation control determines the amount of low frequency oscillator control voltage that is fed to the VCO's and/or the VCF.

THE WHEELS

These are the most common performance control mechanisms currently to be found. They are very simple in operation, consisting of large, serrated plastic discs, about three inches in diameter, that act like edge turn knobs (i.e. the rim becomes the control surface, hence the serrations for grip). (page 87) the pitchbend wheel has a spring-loaded ball and socket arrangement in order that the control can always be returned to the central position when no pitchbend is required. The modulation wheel simply uses the physical extremity of the control as its zero position. Variations have been made on this wheel system: some manufacturers, instead of having a centre notch on the pitchbend wheel, use a spring-return mechanism such that, as the wheel is released, it automatically returns to its initial position.

THE LEVER

This is not a lot different to the wheel, though, instead of there being an edge control, a spring return lever is employed, usually mounted parallel to the keyboard. Often, the lever is used to provide both pitchbend and modulation, in conjunction with a switch system.

THE RIBBON CONTROL

The ribbon control is used primarily as a pitchbend device, though, by the nature of its operation, it can be used as an actual vibrato element. It consists of a short metallic strip, which generates a voltage directly proportional to the point at which it is touched; so, the further away from the centre position, the greater or lesser the voltage, (and hence the pitch), becomes. Natural vibrato is induced by rocking a finger backward and forward on the strip in a fashion similar to a violinist's left hand action. There is available a ribbon controller that replaces the keyboard entirely, generating both control voltage and gate pulses.

THE TOUCH STRIP

This is a similar sort of device to the ribbon controller, save that it bends the note away from the starting position. If you were playing a note on the synthesizer keyboard, and were then to touch the strip at any point, nothing would happen. Only when you slide your finger along the strip does the pitch of the note rise or fall, and when the strip is released, the note reverts to its initial pitch. Clearly, touch strip isn't capable of simple trilling.

THE JOYSTICK

The advantage of the joystick is that it can be used simultaneously, yet independently, to determine the pitchbend and modulation amount. So, in **figure 49,** the pitchbend is controlled by moving the stick in the x-plane (left to right) and modulation is introduced by moving it in the y-plane (up and down). The x-plane movement is normally sprung so that it will return to its central position, whilst moving it upwards will introduce vibrato, and down either trill or noise modulation.

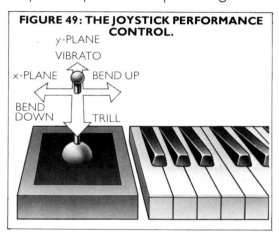

FIGURE 49: THE JOYSTICK PERFORMANCE CONTROL.

y-PLANE
VIBRATO
x-PLANE · BEND UP
BEND DOWN · TRILL

PROPORTIONAL PRESSURE PADS

These are small rubber pads which respond to the pressure applied to them. They are used to bend notes, though it is necessary to have separate pads for up and down pitchbend, and to introduce modulation. They are popular controls because they come closest to actually physically controlling the instrument since you have to actually apply a force rather than simply twiddle or press something.

These are the main types of performance controls that will be encountered. Each has its own advantages and disadvantages; it isn't possible to say that one type of controller is better than another – it is purely a matter of personal taste and you have to find out for yourself which mechanism you best get on with.

THE TOUCH SENSITIVE KEYBOARD

With an electronic organ, the mechanism of the keyboard is simply that of a switch or series of switches being made, or broken. Every time a key is depressed, these switches open or close. A similar arrangement occurs with the keyboard synthesizer. However, because the synthesizer relies heavily on performance controls to increase its expressive powers, the touch sensitive keyboards were developed to provide an additional control medium. Touch sensitive keyboards generate voltages proportional to the way in which the note is played, and this control voltage can then be routed to any voltage controllable parameter.

There are two major types of touch sensitive keyboard:

1) Velocity Sensitive, where the voltage generated when playing a note is proportional to the speed at which the note is depressed – the faster the note is hit, the greater the voltage generated. The mechanism behind this system is fairly simple – when the note is depressed slightly, one contact closes, then, as the key reaches the end of its travel, a second contact closes. The internal circuitry just measures the time between these two contacts closing, and puts out a control voltage proportional to that time;

2) Force Sensitive (sometimes known as second touch), a system that comes into play as the note has reached the end of its travel. Additional pressure at this point will generate a control voltage proportional to the force applied.

It is possible to incorporate both these touch sensitive systems into one instrument, with one voltage being determined by the speed at which the note is depressed, and the second one from the force applied after the note has reached the end of its travel.

Generally speaking, a velocity sensitive control voltage is used to determine the maximum value of the voltage fed to the voltage controlled amplifier – so that the faster a note is played the louder it sounds. Force sensitive control voltages are more often used to introduce pitchbend, or LFO modulation (in particular, vibrato).

Both these control signals are operated in conjunction with an amount control, so that the maximum effect of the velocity/force can be limited to a desired amount.

The term "touch sensitive keyboard" should not be confused with touch responsive, which, generally, refers to a type of keyboard that has no moving parts, i.e. a series of panels arranged in the shape of a conventional keyboard, responding to the touch of a human finger (or whatever). This type of keyboard is very cheap to manufacture, and makes the instrument very small and compact. However, it is fairly difficult to play, and is only really suitable for monophonic synthesizer applications.

PORTAMENTO AND GLISSANDO

One of the most exciting effects possible with a synthesizer is that of portamento/ glissando. You will recall that the controller feeds a control voltage (and a gate/trigger pulse) to the voice module every time a new note is played. This voltage is generally stored in the input circuitry of the voice module until the next note assigned to that module is played. When that happens, the rate at which the previous note's voltage becomes that of the new one can be limited. For example, if a C were to be played on the controller, then the voltage fed to the oscillators might be one volt; if the C an octave above is then played, the oscillator's voltage input would become two volts – but it is possible to adjust the rate at which the control voltage changes between one and two volts. So, instead of making a clean step between voltage levels, the control signal will sweep up (or down) to the new value. This causes the pitch of the oscillator(s) to sweep smoothly between notes at a set rate. Most synthesizers provide this effect with a maximum slew rate of an octave every three seconds, or thereabouts.

Portamento is the correct name for this effect, whereby there is a smooth continuous pitch variation between notes. Glissando is a more complex feature to incorporate into a synthesizer, as it will cause the pitch to step in semitones between notes, again at a variable rate. Glissando, although a very pleasing effect useful for simulations of wind instruments, isn't often encountered because of the relative complexity of the circuitry involved. The portamento/glissando facility can be considered either as part of the voice module, or as part of the controller medium driving it.

3
TYPES OF SYNTHESIZER

KEYBOARD BASED.

Having discussed the subtractive and additive principles of synthesis, and looked in detail at the synthesizer voice module, we can now examine the various different types of synthesizer that use the synthesizer voice module as the sound generation medium, and that employ variations on this theme. Obviously, the design of voice modules varies from instrument to instrument, but the convention of signal flow (VCO-VCF-VCA) is common to almost all subtractive synthesizers.

MONOPHONICS

A monophonic synthesizer is only capable of playing one note at a time – that is to say it has only one voice module. Many players of more traditional keyboards are horrified when they realize that this type of instrument will only play single notes. However, this isn't the problem it might first appear, and, although there is only one note to worry about, the subtleties and expression that can be injected into the sound give the player more than enough scope. Remember that the majority of acoustic instruments, in particular those of the brass and woodwind families, are monophonic.

PRIORITY SYSTEMS

As a monophonic instrument has only one voice generator, everytime a new note is played, then that one voice has to retrigger as the new note. If more than one note is simultaneously played, there has to be a rule of priority as to which note gets assigned to the voice module. There are three main assignment modes to which a synthesizer will conform. Very few instruments offer a choice; it is normally the case that a particular manufacturer will adopt a certain system and stick with it for all his products.

So, if two or more notes are played at any one time:

1) **A LOW NOTE PRIORITY** will cause the lowest note being played to sound.

2) **A HIGH NOTE PRIORITY** will cause the highest note being played to sound.

3) **A LAST NOTE PRIORITY** will assign the voice module to the last note to be played.

Each of these priority assignment modes have inherent advantages and disadvantages, though most players find they can get to grips with any of the three configurations fairly easily. Some players encounter problems with the last note priority system: if a note is played and, just after it has triggered, the key next to it is brushed such that it instantaneously triggers and releases, then, because this note was the last one to be played, it will sound; if the release time is very short, it will die away quickly, even though the first note is still being held. So the player is left holding a note that isn't sounding. Therefore, it is important when using a last note priority system to have a clean playing action.

FULLY VARIABLE SYNTHESIZER

Currently, this is probably the most common form of synthesizer; it is basically a keyboard and a voice module with all the controls present on the control panel, so that each parameter can be set up individually to define the final sound. The best known example of this type of synthesizer must be the **Minimoog,** which has been one of the most popular, fully variable monophonic synthesizers for the past ten years. Production of it ceased only recently. The advantage of the fully variable synthesizer is that all the parameters can be 'user defined' – i.e. you can construct the desired sound completely, though this facility can be a double-edged sword, as, for live performance work, it can be very difficult to accurately change the sound in a hurry.

THE PRESET

Although it may not look so, this instrument employs a synthesizer voice module in the same fashion as the other types of synthesizer. However, as this is a preset instrument, very few of the controls associated with the voice module appear on the front panel. Instead, a series of selector switches are normally to be found within easy reach of the keyboard. These switches are used to select preset "patches" which have been programmed into the instrument at the factory.

When a preset is selected, a series of control voltages and switch data are routed to the various oscillators, filters and amplifiers in such a way that the synthesizer voice module will – or, at least, should – produce a sound not dissimilar to the name given to the preset. So, in a preset synthesizer, the instrument is setting up all the control knobs automatically inside. It is, therefore, a fast and easy instrument to play but this operational ease is counterbalanced by the lack of versatility: the preset synthesizer is generally far less versatile than the fully variable instrument. There are a few overriding controls that can be used to tailor the sound somewhat more to the players own requirements. For example, some preset synthesizers provide a separate brilliance control which is used to move the cut off frequency of the filter, so it is possible to change the timbre of the preset quite dramatically. Most preset synthesizers also have some form of performance controls.

Interestingly, the most common area of use for the preset synthesizer is with the club and home organist, where the instrument is set on top of the organ for additional tonal variations, and lead-line sounds. It is for this reason that so many preset instruments have their selector switches positioned along the panel underneath the keyboard: normally this would make them awkward to use, but, in this instance, their positioning becomes ergonomically ideal. For this reason also, the performance controls are usually of the touch sensitive variety, so that the player can play and modulate/bend with just one hand.

THE PROGRAMMABLE SYNTHESIZER

The programmable synthesizer enjoys the benefits of both the preset and the fully variable instruments, whilst suffering none of their handicaps. A programmable synthesizer is one in which all the voice module controls are available to the player in order to create a specific sound, and when the patch is exactly as desired, all the information regarding the control settings is fed into a memory circuit inside the instrument. This stores the data for recall at a later time. Meanwhile, the player can use the front panel to construct another sound, which can then be put into a different memory location. A programmable synthesizer normally has at least eight such memory locations, so it is possible to store many different patches, all exactly of the sounds required; these can then be recalled as easily as selecting a voice on a preset synthesizer. If it weren't for the fact that programmable synthesizers are quite a lot more expensive than either the fully variable or the preset instruments, then these two latter machines would soon become obsolete.

It isn't a great deal of use having a programmable synthesizer if all the programmed sounds are lost when the instrument is disconnected from the mains. So the designers of these machines use small back-up batteries to power the memory circuits when the instrument is switched off. Today's memories take next to nothing in power, and consequently these batteries can last up to ten years without needing replacement. That being said, programmable instruments have only been around for four or five years, so the ten year lifetime of the batteries hasn't been proved!

The concept of tape dumping has grown up with the programmable synthesizer. Most such instruments use a micro-processor (a small computer) as the central brain for handling all the information and it is a relatively simple operation for the processor to turn all the information regarding the programmed voices into a signal that can be fed into a standard cassette recorder. Many programmables offer this cassette dump facility, whereby the program information can be transferred to tape, leaving the memories free for other patches. When required, the cassette can be replayed into the synthesizer, and the information fed into the memories for recall in the normal way. Many players use this facility to build up a library of sounds.

THE MODULAR SYNTHESIZER

This is the one type of synthesizer that doesn't necessarily conform to the VCO-VCF-VCA signal flow convention (though for most applications this configuration is used). The modular synthesizer is designed so that the various circuit blocks that make up the synthesizer voice module are themselves separate modules that can be arranged or routed as required. The beauty of the modular synthesizer is that the signal routing isn't prepatched – leastways if it is, it can be overridden. The VCOs are separate entities from the VCFs etc, they generally have to be physically patched up – linked together with audio cables, or patch cords. Consequently, this type of instrument is far more versatile.

A modular system is normally housed in a rack mounting unit, which means that separate oscillators, filters etc, can be accommodated to suit the players requirements. For example, if it was required that the output from the oscillators be filtered by three different VCFs, each with a different envelope generator, it would be a simple matter to patch this up – assuming that there were enough VCF and envelope modules available. The modular system is almost exclusively used in the studio, as it does take quite a while to set up a particular sound. It is also a particularly effective instrument when used in conjunction with an analogue sequencer (see Chapter 5). The modular synthesizer is almost always a monophonic instrument.

PEDAL SYNTHESIZERS

The pedal synthesizer is a specialist form of preset instrument that utilizes a pedalboard as the controller as opposed to the normal keyboard. The unit generally sits on the floor and is used to generate synthesized bass voicings. The most famous of this type of instrument is the **Moog Taurus,** which is particularly popular with guitarists requiring sustained, deep, rich notes against which they can solo. They are also used considerably by the more proficient keyboard players – generally those having had a good grounding in pedal technique.

POLYPHONIC SYNTHESIZERS

The standard definition of a polyphonic synthesizer is an instrument with more than one voice module. However, there are several hybrid instruments that do not seem to come under this definition. The above categories of monophonic instrument apply equally to the polyphonic instruments. However, there are additional considerations regarding the way in which the keyboard interfaces with the synthesizer voice modules.

DUOPHONICS

The simplest form of "polyphonic" synthesizer is the duophonic, with just two voice modules. These instruments utilize the low and high note priority systems for each module, so that when two notes are simultaneously held the top one is always assigned to one voice, and the lower note to the other.

VOICE ASSIGNABLES

Ideally, it would be best to have a separate voice module for every note of the keyboard, but for reasons of cost/benefit, this isn't a particularly good policy. So, manufacturers and designers have adopted the voice assignable system, whereby the control circuitry of the instrument routes just the notes being played to a fixed number of synthesizer voice modules. Voice assignable polyphonics generally have between four and sixteen voice modules; it follows that they can only sound as many notes as there are voice modules. As with the monophonics, there is a priority system, though in most cases this is a last note priority, so that every new note played will sound, robbing a voice from one of the notes being held. Polyphonic portamento is possible with this arrangement, but, because it is impossible to have separate sweep rates directly proportional to the length of sweep involved, the effect is different for each note played. Consequently, some notes reach their new destinations long before others; it is, therefore, not a truly valid musical effect.

HOMOGENEOUS AND NON-HOMOGENEOUS VOICE ASSIGNABLES

A polyphonic synthesizer consists of several voice modules. It is generally the case that there is only one set of controls and that these are common to all the voice modules, so that, when the filter cut-off frequency (say) is turned, the filter cut-off point for all the individual voice modules is incremented by an equal amount. This is known as a homogeneous system. When polyphonic synthesizers were first appearing on the market in the mid-Seventies, they often consisted of a bank of voice modules, all fully variable; the keyboard and associated circuitry just assigned an applicable control voltage and gate pulse to them, so it was quite feasible to have a different sound for each voice.

This system, although very versatile, proved to be too unwieldy for most musicians and the homogeneous voice assignable **(figure 50)** took over. More recently, though, a third generation of voice assignables has started to appear. These enable voice modules to be paralleled – they have two sets of voice modules each set with separately programmable voice controls, such that every time a note is played, one voice module from each group is triggered. This enables a far richer, more complex sound to be created and the operation is known as layering.

The most popular type of polyphonic synthesizer is now the programmable voice assignable. (In fact, almost all the larger polyphonics of today have some form of programming facility.) Less common is the preset polyphonic, which, as with its monophonic counterpart, provides a range of pre-programmed sounds quickly and easily, but again, doesn't have the versatility of the programmable instruments. It is necessary, because of the complex assignment operations involved, to use a microprocessor at the heart of a voice assignable instrument; it is therefore logical to make such an instrument programmable, as all the switching circuitry and data handling hardware is already "on board."

The modular polyphonic synthesizer as such, is a rare breed of instrument. One mass manufacturer has recently introduced a polyphonic keyboard controller to be used with a modular system, though demand for such a device isn't great.

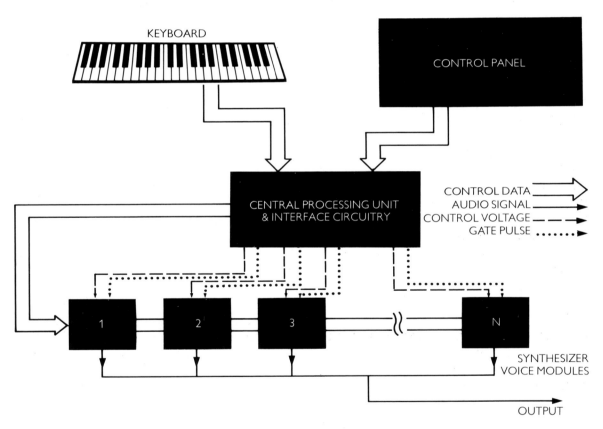

FIGURE 50: HOMOGENEOUS VOICE ASSIGNABLE SYSTEM.

HYBRID POLYPHONICS

The first types of polyphonic synthesizer utilized advanced organ technology, and were fully polyphonic, (i.e. every note could be sounded simultaneously). The **Polymoog** was the forerunner here, and this was the first synthesizer to have specially designed integrated circuits to minimalize the amount of discrete circuitry required. These instruments are generally dual oscillator machines, but instead of having two separate oscillators for each note, (the cost of which would have been prohibitive), two very high frequency voltage controlled oscillators operating at around two million cycles per second, are fed into separate devices known as master tone generators. These act as complex dividers, and each produces the twelve tones, pitched around the 5–10 kHz mark, that make up the chromatic scale. Each of these twenty four (2 x 12) tones are fed through a series of octave (÷2) dividers, in order to derive the pitches required for each note of the entire keyboard. Each note has two independent tones available to it, just like a dual oscillator voice module. These tones are initially square waves (as the dividers act as switches, with two states – on and off), but they are then shaped by the circuitry under each key in order to provide other wave-

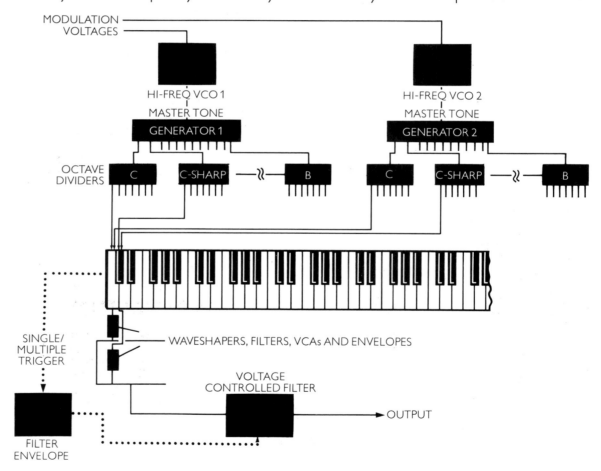

FIGURE 51: FULLY POLYPHONIC MASTER TONE GENERATOR SYSTEM.

forms, which then move through the normal voice module chain. As every note has to have duplicated circuitry, the facilities are generally kept relatively simple. **(See figure 51).**

The problem with using master tone generators is that all the chromatic pitches generated by this device are phase related, so the instrument will sound somewhat flat and lifeless. This problem is alleviated a little by having the two generators running in parallel, as described above. However, the result isn't as pleasing as if each note generated a completely free phase signal. Some manufacturers have attempted to get round this by having twelve or twenty-four top octave voltage controlled oscillators and just using octave dividers to generate the required pitches. In this way, there is no phase relationship between adjoining chromatic pitches.

One major drawback with the fully polyphonic master tone generator system is that it isn't possible to have any form of polyphonic portamento or glide, since the pitches of the notes are firmly related to one another. However, pitchbend and modulation 'en masse' is quite straightforward.

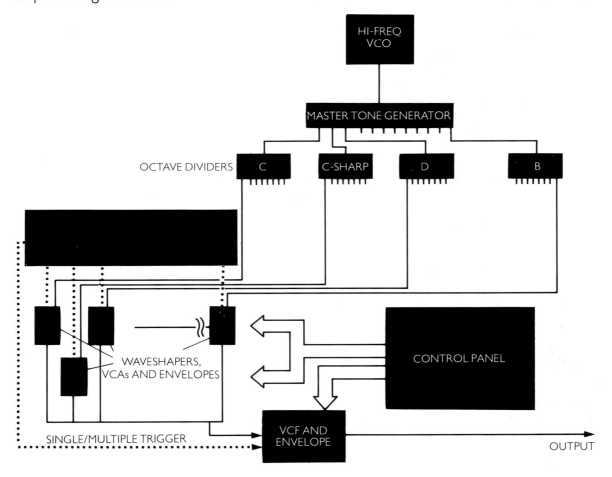

FIGURE 52: PSEUDO-POLYPHONIC SYNTHESIZER.

PSEUDO-POLYPHONICS

There is always a demand for a low cost polyphonic synthesizer, so in order to meet this demand, the pseudo-polyphonic synthesizer was developed. The standard configuration for this type of instrument is shown in **figure 52.** The most costly circuits to manufacture in a synthesizer voice module are the voltage controlled oscillators and filters. So to cut costs, the master tone generator system in conjunction with octave dividers and simple waveshaper circuits provide a relatively inexpensive way in which to generate the pitches. These signals, when triggered by the keyboard, are fed directly into voltage controlled amplifiers in order to have their amplitude shaped; the signals are then mixed together before being fed to a single voltage controlled filter with envelope generator. The signal flow is therefore somewhat different from that of a conventional voice module. As there is only one filter, compromises have to be made in the performance of such an instrument. Either the filter envelope is triggered every time a note is played, or else it only triggers when a new note has been played after all the other keys have been released. So a triggering system was developed – multiple triggering occurring when the envelope is retriggered every time a note is played, and single triggering, only after all the other keys have been released (this is the system adopted by most organ manufacturers for harmonic percussion). Although there is usually a choice between the two types of triggering system on a given instrument, the actual performance of a pseudo-polyphonic synthesizer is restricted by having only one filter, and as a result, the way in which the instrument can be physically played has some limitations. The big benefit of this type of instrument is undoubtedly the reduced cost. Not all pseudo-polyphonics function exactly as detailed here, though the principles are essentially the same.

THE STRING SYNTHESIZER

This term crops up frequently when considering electronic keyboard instruments. However, in the strict sense of the word, this instrument isn't really a synthesizer at all, more a glorified electronic organ. As the name implies, these machines are used to provide simulations of stringed instruments, be they solo violins or full string sections. Their functioning generally relies on one or two master tone generators providing a complete chromatic series of sawtooth waveforms, which are shaped by a relatively simple envelope. The characteristic lush, (though, many say, electronic), string ensemble sound is achieved by feeding the resulting signal through a series of modulators, which serve to delay the signal by various time periods (fractions of seconds) in order to create a much fuller, richer tonal quality. The string machine is becoming less popular these days as the polyphonic synthesizer can produce an equally impressive string simulation, as well as a wide range of other sounds.

ENSEMBLE KEYBOARDS

These generally consist of a combination of different types of electronic keyboard instruments all linked up to one keyboard, though often with the same pitch generation circuitry. The ensemble keyboard instrument will usually include a string section, and a brass or organ section, plus a pseudo-polyphonic synthesizer voice circuitry. Each section has a separate output, and there is an on board mixer to combine the various sections into a single/stereo output. These instruments aren't usually too expensive and they do offer the musician a wide variety of easy-to-use sounds.

OTHER TYPES OF SYNTHESIZER CONTROLLERS

THE GUITAR SYNTHESIZER

Over the past few years, there have been three distinct types of guitar synthesizer. First the guitar control was developed. This sensed which strings and frets were being played and put out a monophonic control voltage and trigger pulse accordingly, to the standard synthesizer voice module. This wasn't a very satisfactory arrangement, as basically it was only a switching device – it didn't utilize any of the control qualities that a guitar can offer, in particular the bending of strings to raise the pitch. The monophonic guitar synthesizer was the next to appear, again providing a single control voltage and trigger output, but deriving this signal from the actual pitch produced by the guitar. The problems associated with this configuration centre around the ability of the pitch-to-voltage converter to track the notes being played. The guitarist must therefore play very cleanly and precisely, making sure that only one note at a time sounds. The control voltage is fed to a standard voice module as before.

The most popular type of guitar synthesizer seems to be the polyphonic, or, more accurately, hexaphonic, models. Here, each string of the guitar generates its own control voltage and gate/trigger pulse. This information is sent down a multi-core cable often to a floor-mounted control unit where all the circuitry is housed. In order to keep costs down, the voltage controlled filter is sometimes shared by the six signal generators. The guitar synthesizer has never been as popular as many manufacturers first expected, and consequently, comparatively little has been done to promote this type of instrument as the logical replacement for the electric guitar.

WIND SYNTHESIZERS

Strange as the concept might seem, the use of a wind-like instrument as a monophonic controller does make a lot of sense. The actual fingering of a wind instrument is easily translated to a control voltage, determining the pitch. However, it is with the wind sensor, (the part that is "blown"), that all the interesting things take place. All the shaping, expression and intonation of the sound produced by a wind instrument come from the mouthpiece, so the wind sensor automatically becomes the amplitude contour generator – the harder one blows, the greater the voltage sent to the VCA – there's no ADSR envelope generator. The synthesizer voice module used is otherwise fairly standard.

PERCUSSION SYNTHESIZERS

These devices simply produce user-determined percussion voices as a response to being struck or hit. They are, in the main, shaped like a small drum, with a series of controls around the edge. Drummers are, as a breed of musician, a fairly conservative group, slow to respond to change, especially if it involves electricity and amplifiers. Consequently, the electronic boom has yet to happen in the percussion market; it seems that only the more adventurous of this fraternity are willing to enter the electronic world.

The most important part of any drum synthesizer is the playing pad, whether it offers both a comfortable response to the drummer playing it, and has the correct dynamic response. When the pad is struck, a control signal is generated proportional to the striking force; it is this signal that is used either to determine the amplitude or the pitch of the sound (or both). An acoustic drum has a very wide dynamic response – i.e. it can be played very softly, or at a deafening level; a good percussion synthesizer should have a correspondingly large dynamic range.

The most commonly heard synthesized percussion voice is the filter (or sometimes oscillator) swoop, which up until fairly recently seemed to appear on every disco recording released.

COMPUTER BASED SYSTEMS

When dealing with voice assignable polyphonic synthesizers (chapter 3.), the use of the microprocessor as the main control element was illustrated. A microprocessor is simply a small computer; it manipulates digital numbers which, in the case of the voice assignable instruments, transmit all the information from the keyboard and control elements, and, if applicable, the programmer memories, to the synthesizer voice modules.

The voice assignable synthesizer, although it normally utilizes a micro-processor, isn't generally considered a true computer system. The computer is primarily used in two main synthesis spheres:

1) **ADDITIVE SYNTHESIS** where the computer is primarily used to construct various voicings by the addition of sine waves.

2) **DIRECT SYNTHESIS** in which the computer, and associated circuitry, actually construct the final output voltage waveform.

Both these systems are in their commercial infancy, and such products as are available are prohibitively expensive for all but the most affluent musicians. It is worthwhile, however, to examine these areas a little further, since rapid technological developments will soon make these instruments more accessible, and, in any case, several recording studios and educational establishments are already equipped with these new generation musical instruments.

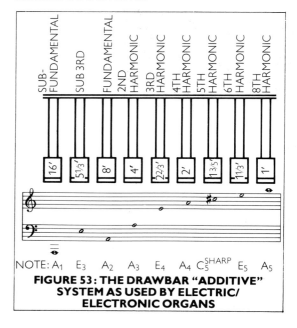

NOTE: A_1 E_3 A_2 A_3 E_4 A_4 C_5^{SHARP} E_5 A_5

FIGURE 53: THE DRAWBAR "ADDITIVE" SYSTEM AS USED BY ELECTRIC/ ELECTRONIC ORGANS

ADDITIVE SYNTHESIS

We saw in chapter 1 how the various different periodic waveforms were made up of sine waves with varying frequencies and amplitudes; additive synthesis works the other way – sine waves of different frequencies and amplitudes are added together to construct not only the basic periodic waveforms, but indeed any waveform at all. The simplest form of additive synthesizer could be considered to be the old drawbar organ **(figure 53).** Here, each drawbar provides a separate harmonically related sinewave, so that a very wide variety of complex wave forms could be constructed by various combinations of the settings of the nine drawbars. This is, however, a static arrangement, and the computer based systems operate a much more involved process. Obviously, in order to create involved polyphonic waveforms, a large number of analogue sine wave generators are required, each with variable pitch and amplitude. In order to coordinate the summation of these harmonics and overtones, computer control is required, and this facilitates the creation of very complex sounds.

With subtractive synthesis, the main performance restriction is the timbral control. All acoustic instruments have a continuously varying harmonic spectrum, so a voltage controlled filter with (at best) an ADSR envelope is a compromise. With a computer based additive system, the harmonic content of a sound can be specified for every instant in time, and each integral time period can, if necessary, have a completely different structure to the previous element. It now becomes clear why a computer is needed to keep things under control. The limitations of an additive system are dictated by the number of sinusoidal (sine wave) generators available, and the clocking speed of the computer (i.e. how fast it can process all the information). Such a system can, in essence, be represented quite simply **(figure 54).** Notice that there is no need for any filters, or any final VCA envelope generator, because the only parameters that need to be defined are the pitch and amplitude of all the harmonic generators.

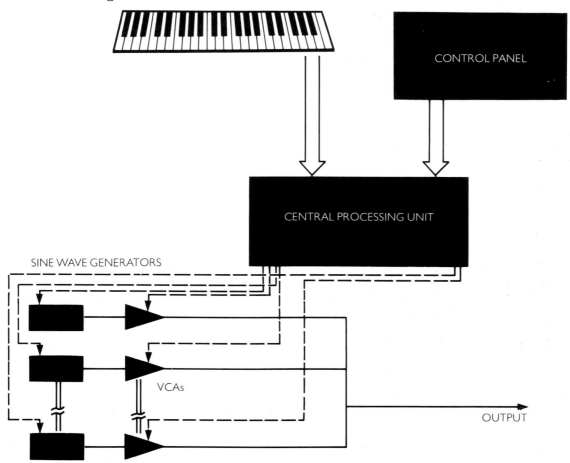

FIGURE 54: TYPICAL ADDITIVE SYSTEM.

With a computer at one's disposal, many other features are normally included in an additive system. First, the instrument can easily be polyphonic, and is generally used as such; polyphonic operation just limits the number of generators available for each note. Second, most computer systems have advanced information storage systems (floppy discs, and the like) so it is possible to build up complete multi-channel compositions purely within the instrument, without the aid of tape recorders. The computer will file away all the different voicing information (not the sound itself), though again, the number of generators serves as the limiting factor. A third, and rather exciting feature of these instruments is the signal sampling system that several models provide. This will sample any external signal, and re-create it using the voice generators. For example, a note played on an oboe could be fed into the analyser section, and the computer would generate a simulation that could be played back at any pitch – polyphonically even.

DIRECT SYNTHESIS

These instruments, although they have yet to make their mark, are set to become the most important musical instruments of the Eighties. Instead of providing control signals to program analogue generators, the computer is here used to create the final output wave-form directly. **Figure 55(a)** represents, as an example of the operation, a square wave of 200 Hz, and **(b)** a sawtooth wave of 300 Hz which is a perfect fifth (just intonation) above the square wave. **Figure 55 (c)** illustrates the combined waveform of these non-phase related signals. Now, it is a simple task to represent this composite waveform by a string of numbers, each referring to the voltage level at a particular instant in time – giving us a numeric representation of the signal. These numbers can be turned into binary numbers ("1"s and "0"s) that the computer can understand, and this is the simple principle on which direct synthesizers operate. However, instead of receiving, it generates them, and a device known as a digital-to-analogue converter translates these numbers into the voltage waveform. So, there are no filters, amplifiers or oscillators as such; the signal is generated inside the computer from the information provided via the keyboard and control panel, and from all the programming instructions given it as to how to interpret the information.

As yet, technology isn't quite advanced enough to make these commonplace instruments – a fairly powerful computer is required, with a very fast processing time, and the player must have a good knowledge of computer programming. Given a few years, the situation will undoubtedly be very different.

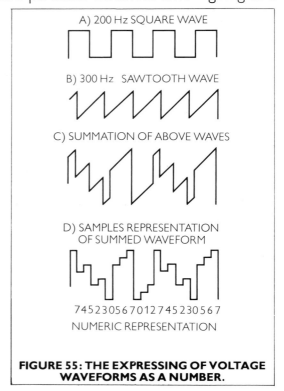

A) 200 Hz SQUARE WAVE

B) 300 Hz SAWTOOTH WAVE

C) SUMMATION OF ABOVE WAVES

D) SAMPLES REPRESENTATION OF SUMMED WAVEFORM

7 4 5 2 3 0 5 6 7 0 1 2 7 4 5 2 3 0 5 6 7
NUMERIC REPRESENTATION

FIGURE 55: THE EXPRESSING OF VOLTAGE WAVEFORMS AS A NUMBER.

SOME COMMERCIAL INSTRUMENTS

FULLY VARIABLE MONOPHONIC – THE SEQUENTIAL CIRCUITS PRO-ONE

This is a relatively new instrument, first appearing at the beginning of 1981. Sequential Circuits, Inc. are a California-based synthesizer manufacturing company, and this instrument marks their first low cost monophonic product.

The Pro-One, as it is monophonic, has only one voice module, and, as it is a fully variable instrument, all the controls relating to the voice module appear on the front panel.

OSCILLATORS: This is a dual oscillator synthesizer. Oscillator A provides a ramp and a pulse waveform, whilst Oscillator B will generate a ramp, triangle and a pulse wave. Slide switches are used to select the waveshapes, so it is possible to combine different waveforms. Both oscillators have a continually variable frequency control, as well as octave stepping switches. Synchronization is possible, simply by flicking a switch, whence oscillator A will lock onto the harmonics of oscillator B. Oscillator B can be switched into low frequency mode whence its output, (which includes the triangle wave), can be used to modulate another parameter. Oscillator B can also be disconnected from the keyboard control voltage.

AUDIO MIXER: This has separate level controls for Oscillators A and B, whilst a third knob either introduces noise, or is used to set the threshold level for an external signal. This means that, every time an external signal applied to an instrument reaches a certain amplitude (the threshold), a trigger pulse is generated, which fires the envelopes. This makes the Pro-One a useful instrument for processing external signals.

FILTER: This is a 24 dB/octave low pass type. There is a separate keyboard track control which determines how the cut off frequency is going to vary with the note played. The filter has its own ADSR envelope generator.

AMPLIFIER: Again, the VCA has its own envelope generator (ADSR).

MODULATION: The Pro-One has a most comprehensive modulation system, which enables various different control signals to be routed to any of five different destinations.

PERFORMANCE CONTROLS: These consist of two wheels to the left of the keyboard. The far left wheel has a centre dente, as it is used for pitchbending, whilst the other, (the modulation amount wheel), is used in conjunction with the above modulation section.

THE KEYBOARD: Three octaves (37-notes) C to C. There is no touch sensitivity.

ARPEGGIATOR & SEQUENCER: The Pro-One is one of the few synthesizers that incorporates a sequencer, and arpeggiator. The sequencer will store up to forty notes and play them back, though when it does so, they are all of equal duration. The arpeggiator almost enables the Pro One to function as a polyphonic instrument. By playing a chord, all the notes will sound in turn; the rate at which each note is triggered is determined by the low frequency oscillator. The arpeggiator is particularly useful for providing rhythmic accompaniments.

MODULAR – THE ROLAND 100M SYSTEM

The Roland 100-M system is probably the most popular modular system currently available. This is due, primarily, to its relatively low cost, and the high quality and performance of the modules. Being a modular system, it offers the players a number of options as to which modules to include in his instrument. It also gives him the possibility of extending his system at a later date. The 100-M consists of a keyboard, a rack, and a series of modules.

THE KEYBOARD: In this instance, it is a four octave monophonic type with performance controls – pitchbend, glide, and transposition – situated alongside. Other types of keyboard are available for use with the 100-M system, including a four output polyphonic model (four sets of gates and control voltage outputs are available for driving the various oscillators etc.).

THE RACK: This is used to house the various modules. It also contains the power supply for driving the modules and keyboard. Obviously, it would be ridiculous to have each module individually plugged into the domestic mains supply. Along the lower panel of the rack are a series of jack sockets which are grouped together in order to split up signals; for example, a signal can be fed in via one of the sockets, and there are then three output feeds that can be taken off to other parts of the instrument for modifying, processing, and so on.

THE MODULES: Each module generally contains a section of the synthesizer voice module. Typical modules contain: dual voltage controlled oscillators (two), dual voltage controlled filters, dual voltage controlled amplifiers, two envelope generators, a low frequency oscillator, etc. Certain more specialized types are available including, a phasing/chorus module, and an analogue sequencer.
    The signal flow from one module to another is determined using mini jack leads. There is access to almost every conceivable stage of the signal processing, so it is possible to build up varied and complex patch arrangements.

POLYPHONIC PROGRAMMABLE VOICE ASSIGNABLES – THE OBERHEIM OB-XA

The OB-Xa is an American product that first appeared in the spring of 1981. It is a voice assignable polyphonic with the capability of layering voice modules. The OB-Xa is available with varying numbers of voice modules, although the instrument is normally purchased as an eight voice synthesizer.

THE KEYBOARD: A full five octaves. This is a minimum requirement for an instrument of this nature. The keyboard can be split (electronically) into two sections at any point, such that half the voice modules are assigned to one part of the keyboard, and the remainder to the other.

THE VOICE MODULES: Each module consists of two voltage controlled oscillators, a voltage controlled low pass filter (24 dB/octave or 12 dB/octave – switchable), two ADSR envelope generators, a voltage controlled amplifier, and a low frequency oscillator. There is just one set of controls common to all the modules, so this is a homogeneous system.

THE PROGRAMMER: This is used to store the information required to set up the voice modules in order to create specific sounds. The OB-Xa has thirty-two different memory locations, so thirty-two different sounds/effects can be stored and recalled at the touch of a button. In addition, eight different programme combinations can be recorded. This means that half the voice modules can be given the information to produce one sound, whilst the remaining modules produce another. The modules can then either be layered, whereby every time a note is pressed, two modules each producing different sounds, are triggered; or the keyboard is split and the modules detailed as previously mentioned. The layering facility enables the OB-Xa to construct far more complex sounds than would be possible with a "one voice per note" instrument.

PERFORMANCE CONTROLS: The OB-Xa uses the lever system. These levers are sprung so that they return exactly to their centre position on release; they provide control over pitchbend and modulation amount, and, in conjunction with a series of push-button switches, the control signals are routed to the various parts of the instruments circuitry. The OB-Xa also features polyphonic portamento which can be particularly effective with an instrument of this ilk, especially as it has such a characteristically powerful sound.

69

PRESET – THE TEISCO S-100P

The S-100P is a monophonic preset synthesizer, consequently it has only the one voice module, and in this case, it is of the single VCO variety. Most of the controls associated with the fully variable synthesizer have been replaced by a series of selector switches located just beneath the keyboard. These set the preset voicings. Each tab has three positions: Centre – off; Up – selecting one voicing; and Down – another. The presets cannot be combined with one another, so priority is given to the one furthest to the left. The preset voicings include simulations of most acoustic instruments, from Tuba and Hawaiian Guitar, through to Piano and Piccolo. In addition, there are several electronic, or "synthe" sounds as well as such esoteric voicings as "Whistle," "Waves," "Voices," and "Wind."

The keyboard is touch sensitive, such that the harder the key is pressed, the greater the effect on the pitchbend, brilliance, vibrato, or growl. The Teisco S-100P also features a built-in reverberation spring, which adds depth to the sound, and a Flanger circuit, which produces a spatial effect somewhere in between phasing, and chorus.

4
USING THE SYNTHESIZER

By now, you should be familiar with the "nuts and bolts" of the synthesizer, so in this chapter we will look at the way in which the synthesizer is used either to simulate existing instruments, or to create original sounds and effects. We will therefore look at synthesizer applications that can be grouped under two headings: **IMITATIVE,** and **ABSTRACT (OR IMAGINATIVE).**

In order to capture the qualities of any sound, the synthesist has to be on the ball, knowing what parameters are going to have what effect on the final sound. It's a bit like trying to play by ear; to get it sounding right, the chords and melody have to be correctly structured.

Obviously, the better the synthesizer being used, the more avenues of approach that will be open to the player. But, even the most basic instrument will provide the opportunity to simulate most existing instruments, and to produce a wide range of special sounds.

IMITATIVE SYNTHESIS

THE HARMONIC STRUCTURE APPROACH

We have seen how the harmonics of a sound come together to determine its overall character. Well, one way to simulate that sound is to analyze its harmonic structure, and to try and re-create the sound using the technology available – your synthesizer. For example, **figure 56** shows the harmonic structure of a steady state open violin string. As can be clearly seen, the second harmonic is predominant – even stronger than the fundamental. If we look at the structures of the common oscillator waveforms, we see that there's not much that corresponds to the violin's series; so, we would have to use the low pass filter, and, (if there's one available), the high pass filter, and any other tricks we can, to make an approximation to this signal. The sawtooth wave has a vague similarity to part of the violin's series (that is, without the fundamental's attenuation). So we could either use the high pass filter on the sawtooth wave in order to reduce the relative amplitude of the fundamental, or, if we have a synthesizer with a dual oscillator voice module and a synchronization facility (see chapter 2),

we could introduce a separate fundamental by setting oscillator 1 onto the second harmonic producing a sawtooth wave; the second oscillator could be used to generate a sine (or more probably a triangle) wave to act as the fundamental an octave below oscillator 1. This is fine, except that the small seventh and large twelfth harmonics are still causing problems.

In fact, this is all getting too complicated, and we are getting into the realms of the way in which manufacturers program preset synthesizers. It's true that the harmonic structure of the sound to be imitated is important, but most players aren't in the position to carry out complex harmonic surveys on existing

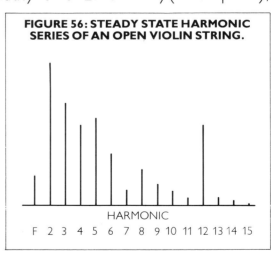

FIGURE 56: STEADY STATE HARMONIC SERIES OF AN OPEN VIOLIN STRING.

HARMONIC
F 2 3 4 5 6 7 8 9 10 11 12 13 14 15

sounds in order to produce accurate simulations. This is especially so when we are primarily concerned with subtractive, rather than additive synthesis.

SELECTING CHARACTERISTICS

The secret of imitative synthesis is to be able to pick out the characteristic nuances of a sound and to re-create them – the rest isn't nearly as important as might be expected.

Consider a violin passage: what are the most important qualities relating to the violin's sound? Believe it or not, they are modulation, and the attack time of the amplifier envelope. This can be shown experimentally, with the oscillator set to a mid frequency sawtooth wave, the filter cut-off frequency set very high, no filter modulation and the VCA envelope arranged to give a fairly slow attack time, sustain on full, and a relatively fast release time. Delayed frequency modulation should be used, (or, alternatively, a vibrato modulation should be gently introduced by means of the performance control, or a relevant control knob/slider), after a second or so of any sustained note.

When a few notes are played, the characteristic solo violin sound can be heard. The delayed modulation is responsible for bringing this sound to life. If the waveform is changed to a pulse wave, the overall sound will be different, but the effect still convincing. However, if the attack time, which was somewhat sluggish, is changed, then the legato violin effect would be instantly destroyed. Obviously, other parameters are important – a sine wave *won't* produce a convincing string sound, as there are no harmonics present at all. By picking out these prime parameters of a sound, the imitative synthesist is half-way there. The main point that should be grasped at this stage is that, even though a certain synthesizer may be very basic in terms of the features and facilities it offers, a considerable amount can be achieved if the sound to be simulated is analyzed – not technically, but by the brain – before an attempt is made to reconstruct it.

PLAYING STYLE

Even the most expensive and prestigious polyphonic synthesizers won't sound "right" if straight triads are played for all the voicings. It is essential to voice the notes that are being played (in the musical sense) to suit the instrument being simulated. For example, when trying to create the sound of a string ensemble, it is necessary to pull the chords apart, (i.e. to have cellos sounding in one register, violas and violins in others), and instead of playing straight chords, try to keep each part separate. For example, if you listen to a flute section, you won't hear them playing block chords (at least you are unlikely to), so when simulating flutes using a polyphonic synthesizer, split your playing into parts, as if two or three flutes were each playing a separate, distinct line. That being said, if you've ever listened to "Strawberry Fields Forever" by The Beatles, you will have noticed that the initial flute voicings are played almost as block chords, and it sounds most strange. This passage was played on a **Mellotron** (a glorified tape player, with a separate magnetic tape for each key). So, there are no hard and fast rules in music. However, to get a *realistic* (flute) voicing, it is important to capture the sprightliness of the acoustic instrument, and, if playing more than one part, to try to keep one voice for the melody, whilst the second, and subsequent voices play a counterpoint.

When imitating other instruments, it is easy to make obvious mistakes; a common error is to play in a manner that would be impossible for that instrument. If we return to our flute example, then introducing portamento really wouldn't add to the air of realism simply because a flute cannot glide between notes; a glissando, whereby the frequency of the VCO steps in semitones between the two notes is fine, because a flute is physically capable of such a manoeuvre. On the other hand, a trombone will employ the glide facility, and not the glissando. Similarly, a flute voicing isn't going to have a sine (or triangle) wave vibrato, so use a square wave to modulate the frequency, thus providing a trill effect when necessary.

We will now examine ways in which various acoustic and electric instruments can be simulated using the synthesizer. These are just meant as rough guidelines as to the approach to take. Some people may have different ways in which to simulate these instruments; it is often a matter of personal preference. But remember – every instrument has its own distinct peculiarities which can be used by the synthesist to fool the listener as to exactly what he is hearing.

SOLO VIOLIN: Use a single oscillator (two only if they are synchronized) with the filter almost fully open, and with the amplitude envelope set with an attack time of between a quarter and half second, full sustain, and a fast release time. A sawtooth wave is probably the best to use, and should be done so with frequency modulation from the sine or triangle wave output of the LFO. Alternatively, some prefer to use a pulse width modulated rectangular wave. It is most important that the release time is set fairly fast when using a polyphonic synthesizer, otherwise the notes will run into one another destroying the solo effect. If the synthesizer has a release footswitch, a longer release time can be added, if necessary, to the last note of a phrase.

SOLO VIOLA AND 'CELLO: Use a similar technique as above, but pitch the oscillators down into a lower register. The 'cello has a greater acoustic inertia than the violin, so it may be necessary to increase the attack time a little.

STRING ENSEMBLE: Again, sawtooth waves with frequency modulation, or rectangular waves with pulse width modulation should be used. The release time of the VCA envelope should also be longer. If a dual oscillator machine is being used, then the oscillators should be set slightly out of tune with one another, thus providing a much more full, lush sound, without exhibiting the mushy timbre that electronic chorus modulators tend to impart on the sound of string synthesizers. If a single oscillator instrument is being used, it is best to use a pulse width modulated source signal.

BRASS: The main characteristic of a brass sound is the increase and decrease in the harmonic content of the sound as the note progresses. The usual way in which to tackle this simulation is to take the sawtooth output from the oscillator(s) and then to have the filter sweep it with a fastish attack time, and with the decay/release following the amplitude of the note. The exact positioning of the filter cut-off frequency is very important, so it is essential to experiment. The VCA envelope needs to have a fast attack and release time, with the sustain level near maximum. Brass lines are either very punchy, or mellow and sustained, so the part has to be played accordingly. Often, it can be very effective to use the oscillators of a dual oscillator voice module synthesizer set a fifth apart. This tends to increase the harmonic content of the signal quite dramatically, and give the filter something to really work on. It is necessary, though, to be careful when using this arrangement on a polyphonic synthesizer, as certain chords will cause some dissonance.

FLUTE: The triangle wave output from the oscillator is the best starting point for producing a flute sound although a sine wave, from the filter in oscillation, can be used. However, the harmonics of the triangle wave can be used to provide a hint of a chiff (the breathy attack phase) if the envelope controls are juggled. The VCA envelope should have a fairly fast attack time – though not too fast, otherwise the smoothness of the flute's character will be destroyed. If, as mentioned earlier, you do play block chords using a polyphonic flute voicing, then the output will sound somewhat like a steam calliope.

HUMAN VOICE/CHOIR: The important characteristic of the human voice revolves around the relationship between the attack of a note and the pitch: the human voice tends to start slightly flat, and then to slew up into the note. So in order to get a realistic simulation of a vocal sound, a control known as a bender should be used. Unfortunately, very few instruments incorporate this device, so it will probably be the case that you will have to improvize. The amount of bend required is minimal – a quarter-tone or less. The oscillators should, therefore, be de-tuned by that amount and then the filter (or VCA) envelope control voltage used to bring the instrument into tune as the note is played. By using a sawtooth wave, modulated by a sine (or triangle) wave, and juggling around with the filter, (the resonance being quite well advanced), it is possible to get a smooth vocal sound. The bend effect can be introduced by using the performance control, but, as such a small pitch change is involved, it can become quite tricky.

ELECTRIC AND ELECTRONIC ORGANS: It is possible, using a dual oscillator synthesizer, to produce a close approximation to both a tone-wheel organ *(Hammond)* and something more reminiscent of the old *Vox Continental.* To stimulate the Hammond sound, the filter should be set for high resonance, and the beating between the two oscillators, set up to produce sawtooth outputs, making an effective re-creation of the rotary cabinet effect. Additionally, if the filter is closed down then modulated by a short percussive envelope, the familiar key clicks of these old instruments can be included.

    The Vox Continental type sound requires quite a different approach. Here the prime factors are the rich harmonic content (each drawbar producing a waveshape more akin to a sawtooth wave) and the vibrato. So, if both oscillators are set up to provide sawtooth waves, and tuned two octaves apart, then you have a sound fairly rich in harmonics. The filter should be fully open, and the envelopes set to give a straight on-off shape. Both oscillators should be frequency modulated with a sine or triangle wave from the LFO. When this modulating waveform is introduced, the character of the voicing instantly takes on that "House Of The Rising Sun" quality.

These are just some examples of the imitative possibilities of the synthesizer and there are very few instruments that cannot be re-created to some extent.

KORG   **MINI MOOG**

ABSTRACT (OR IMAGINATIVE) SYNTHESIS

Few people use the synthesizer solely for creating simulations of existing instruments; they want to create their *own* sounds. However, after the initial knob twiddling period, most players settle down with just a handful of their favourite stock sounds. In order to get the most out of a synthesizer, the full potential of the instrument must be realized. Abstract synthesis relies on being able to get as much out of the instrument as possible. There is very little that can be said on the subject as it relies so heavily on the imagination and playing style of the musician; however the next few paragraphs serve to illustrate some of the possibilities that many synthesizers offer, and that are all too seldom tapped.

First, some very strange, yet musical effects can be achieved by high frequency modulating the filter, using a sine or triangle wave from one of the audio oscillators. This should be running at over 2 kHz, and used in conjunction with the filter envelope generator and filter keyboard track. If an envelope with a fast attack time and slow release time is used, the resulting effect is very similar to that of a voice box.

Harmonic percussion effects can be most effective, though these are only possible if playing a dual oscillator voice module based synthesizer. Oscillator 1 (say) is used as the root, whilst oscillator 2 is set either two, or two-and-a-half octaves higher. The filter is then used to shape the evelope of oscillator 2 without having much effect on the root note, which in turn is shaped by the VCA and associated envelope generator. If the filter has a fast attack time and a relatively fast decay, then a nice percussive effect is obtained. However, by giving it a long attack time, it is possible to create a building effect, with the sound growing in harmonic content as the filter envelope lets oscillator 2 sound through.

It is a worthwhile experiment to set up the oscillators at strange intervals apart, especially if the synthesizer is equipped with a synchronization feature. This will give a wave-form with a much richer harmonic content, and thus increase the power of the filter.

The ADSR envelope is a very important tool, as not only will it shape the contour of a note, but, in certain circumstances, it will also provide a degree of control over the length of the note, dependent on how the key/note is played. For example, if the controls are set up as shown in **figure 57,** by playing in a pizzi-cato fashion (the note being quickly triggered and released), the envelope will jump to the release phase without taking any notice of the decay time control, and, in this instance, the note will have a long release time. If, however, the note is played and held, as there is no sustain level and the decay time is very fast, the note will die away quickly. So in effect, the playing style associated with a more conven-

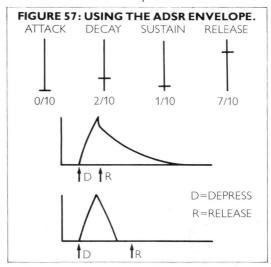

FIGURE 57: USING THE ADSR ENVELOPE.

ATTACK   DECAY   SUSTAIN   RELEASE

0/10   2/10   1/10   7/10

D=DEPRESS

R=RELEASE

tional keyboard instrument, (i.e. a piano), is reversed – holding a note will kill it, and quickly releasing it will cause it to die away slowly. This is quite a useful trick, as it enables an extra degree of control to be achieved from the keyboard playing style.

Don't be afraid to play around with the controls of the synthesizer whilst holding or playing a run of notes: the performance control section is obviously designed for changing certain parameters whilst playing the instrument. However, there is nothing to stop the player altering other parameters whilst performing. For example, the attack time of the note can be varied, completely changing the character of the sound, or the resonance can be adjusted. Experiment with new sounds and new ways of injecting expression into the playing.

5
SYNTHESIZER ACCESSORIES

This chapter deals with the various ancillary equipment that is often used in conjunction with the synthesizer. One of the beauties of a voltage controlled system is that the voltages can originate not only from within the synthesizer, but also from an external source. There is, therefore, a great deal of potential for the use of various voltage producing accessories. The other type of equipment that will be discussed is used to process the final output of the synthesizer. Various sound-enhancing devices can be used to great effect.

THE SEQUENCER

This is probably the most important of the synthesizer accessories, so we'll look closely at its function and operation. Basically, a sequencer is a device that produces chains of user-determined control voltages that are sequentially used to control automatically certain parameters of the synthesizer voice module(s). The sequencer is a spin-off, a by-product that has evolved out of the synthesizer. The first thing to establish is that a sequencer is totally useless without a synthesizer – on its own, it can do nothing, as, essentially, it is just a special type of controller. It's a bit like having a tape deck – it isn't much use without an amplifier and speakers, or headphones. The comparison to a tape machine runs much deeper, as we will see shortly.

A sequencer's main use is to "play" bass patterns, melody lines and special effects, as it has been told to by the player. It is a two-way device: information has to be put into it regarding when and what voltages are to be put out, and these control signals can be called upon as and when necessary to drive the synthesizer. The sequencer is primarily used to set the control voltage of the oscillators and to trigger the envelope generators, but it can be used to drive any voltage controllable parameter as desired.

The subject of sequencers can be a rather confusing one, as there are so many different types available. However, there are two distinct varieties that can be considered separately: the Analogue, and the Digital sequencers.

THE ANALOGUE SEQUENCER

Analogue sequencers were the first on the commercial scene; they were "on stream" almost directly the first synthesizers became available to the general public. They are comparatively simple to understand, though to get the most out of them, it is important to realize their full capabilities. **Figure 58** shows a simplified version of what you can expect to find on the front panel of one of these devices. Note that there are three rows of eight control knobs. Each of these rows is known as a channel and there is a separate voltage output for each channel (A, B, and C, in this case).

In the figure, each channel has eight steps or stages – so, for each stage there are three independent voltage outputs. The sequencer simply steps through each stage and puts out the three independent channel voltages that correspond to the control knob setting for that stage. The position of the sequence is usually indicated by a small light (a light emitting diode) under that step. The sequencer illustrated would be defined as an eight-stage, three-channel analogue model.

The term analogue refers to the use of the voltage in a direct manner, i.e. it is possible to rotate one of the control knobs on the sequencer, and to vary the voltage continuously from zero volts up to five volts (say), though the term has grown in this context to encompass the process whereby the player constructs the sequence, step by step, using separate controls for each function and stage.

In our illustrated example, there are other controls for determining the speed at which the sequence is played back; a rotary switch is usually included to set the length of the sequence, (that is the number of steps required), so in this case we can have up to eight. When the end of the sequence is reached, the unit will normally reset to the

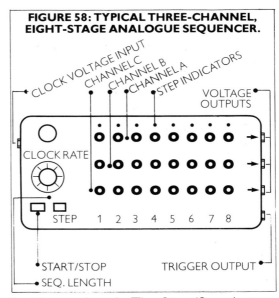

FIGURE 58: TYPICAL THREE-CHANNEL, EIGHT-STAGE ANALOGUE SEQUENCER.

first stage so that the sequence will repeat itself without a break. The Start/Stop button simply does as it says – starts and stops the sequence – whilst the Step button is used to move manually from one stage to the next, which is useful for setting up sequences.

Figure 59 gives a clearer idea as to how the sequencer can be used, and how it is linked up to a synthesizer. The first consideration is whether the sequencer is compatible with the given synthesizer. They both must utilize the same type of trigger pulse (or gate), and ideally they should be designed for the same voltage-pitch ratio (for example 1 volt per octave). Pitch, timbre and volume are of fundamental importance to a sound, so a sequencer is often best suited to an instrument that offers control voltage inputs to the voltage controlled oscillator (VCO), the voltage controlled filter (VCF), and the voltage controlled amplifier (VCA). Undoubtedly, the most satisfactory type of synthesizer for interfacing with a sequencer is a modular type, although many other types of synthesizer offer these facilities.

The analogue sequencer will function with both polyphonic and monophonic synthesizers provided that they have the necessary control voltage inputs. However, when using a polyphonic instrument, the sequencer is generally assigned one of the voice modules only, leaving the instrument to otherwise function normally, so the sequencer can be used to produce a single bass/melody line against which the other voices can be played. Some synthesizers do not have a full compliment of control voltage inputs, but as long as there is a voltage input to the oscillators, the sequencer will still be of use.

The analogue sequencer can, in the example shown, be used in place of a controller or keyboard as, instead of a line being played on the keyboard, the sequencer is doing all the work, leaving the player's hands free either to modify the sound on the synthesizer's control panel, or to play against the sequence on another instrument.

We haven't as yet discussed the firing of the synthesizers envelope generators. There is a link between synthesizer and sequencer that carries the gate/trigger pulse indicating when a new step is to sound. That is, each time the sequencer moves to a new "note," a new pulse is sent down the line to the envelope generators – just in the same way that the keyboard generated a pulse everytime a new note is played.

FIGURE 59: TYPICAL SEQUENCER/SYNTHESIZER INTERFACE.

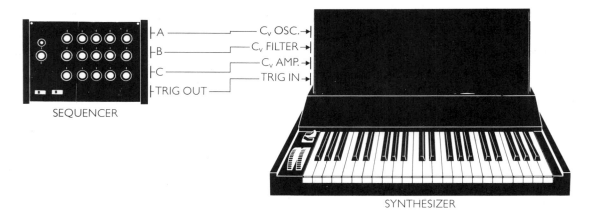

FIGURE 60: SEQUENCER/SYNTHESIZER INTERFACE WITH KEYBOARD TRANSPOSITION AND STEP TIME CONTROL.

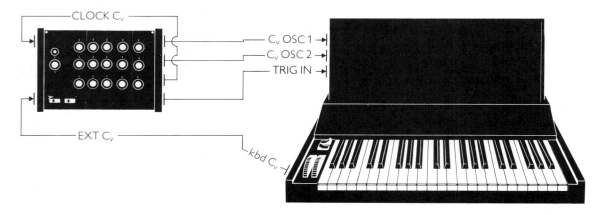

FIGURE 61: DIGITAL SEQUENCER/SYNTHESIZER INTERFACE.

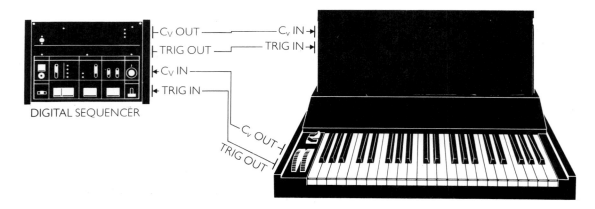

The setting up of a sequence is quite straightforward; in our example, it would be best to open fully both the VCF and VCA, so that a continuous note is heard; then, simply step through each note of the sequence, setting the pitch via Channel A's control knobs. Once this is set, the filter cut off frequency for each note can be set using Channel B, and finally the relative amplitude is set up on Channel C. Note that the filter and amplitude envelope generators are still operative – the filter merely adjusts their bias.

If we were to play back the sequence as shown in **figure 59,** it would become apparent that all the notes were of the same length. For many applications, this is not a problem. However, some sequencers are designed such that a low frequency voltage controlled oscillator is used to step automatically through the sequence, as opposed to an ordinary LFO. The advantage of this can be seen by considering **figure 60.** Here, the voltage of Channel C is being fed back into the control voltage input of the voltage controlled stepping oscillator – more commonly known as the clock. So, for a certain step, if the voltage for Channel C were increased, this in turn would cause the clock frequency to increase and, consequently, the sequence would step more quickly to the next stage, where, if Channel C's voltage were less, the duration of that stage would be increased. Therefore, Channel C is now being used to control the relative timing of the sequence. Several machines have this facility hard wired, so that it isn't necessary to connect a lead from the output back to the clock input; merely flicking a switch will make the circuit internally.

Figure 60 also shows a couple of other changes. First, the synthesizer in the example is a dual oscillator type, so Channel A has been patched to VCO 1, and Channel B to VCO 2. This enables a pseudo-chord sequence to be set up using the synthesizer voice module; both oscillators *sound* simultaneously, though they can be *pitched* independently.

A further link has been made between the two devices, which can be used to provide some of the most pleasing effects, using the synthesizer's controller to pitch the entire sequence. The control voltage output from the synthesizer is fed to the summing input of the sequencer. This results in channels A and B being incremented by the control voltage, so the sequence will be automatically transposed to the key played on the synthesizer's controller. This is an effect regularly used on the rhythm tracks of disco records. Some synthesizers are designed such that this link isn't necessary; in other words, the keyboard (controller) is always linked to the oscillator inputs, even when an external control voltage is used.

THE DIGITAL SEQUENCER

Whereas the player "talks" to the analogue sequencer which in turn passes information to the synthesizer, with the digital sequencer, the information flow is slightly different. Here, the sequencer monitors what is being played on the keyboard (controller) of the synthesizer, and stores that information in its memory until it is required to feed it back to a synthesizer voice module. The digital sequencer can be considered to be rather like a tape recorder, but, instead of recording audio signals, voltages and trigger pulses are stored, and instead of using magnetic tape, the information is retained in silicon chips known as random access memories (RAMs).

Unlike the analogue sequencer, digital devices are far more immediate. A pattern is played on the synthesizer keyboard and the control voltages and trigger pulses generated are fed into the sequencer's memory. The sequence is then replayed and this control information is fed straight back to the synthesizer, normally to control the oscillators, and triggering of envelopes, as if the keyboard were being played straight off.

Because the digital sequencer memorizes not only the pitch (voltage) of the note but also the time until the next note, the sequence will not consist of equally spaced notes, i.e. it can be said to be a real time sequence. Obviously, though, the longer each note sounds, the more memory is used up. So, in order to conserve memory (which is relatively expensive), many digital sequencers have something like a seven second limit to the duration of a note. When a note is held for longer than this, a light normally comes on, and that note will be only seven seconds long when the sequence is replayed at normal speed.

Of course, different models employ different systems, but this limiting mode seems to be the most common. If it is necessary to play notes with longer duration than the seven second limit, the tempo control can be adjusted so that the sampling of the sequence is slower. However, this means that if very short notes are played, the sequencer may not be able to pick them up fast enough, and they may not appear in the recorded sequence.

Several manufacturers split up the sequence memory into several separate memory banks of sixteen, twenty-four, forty-eight, (or whatever), notes' length, so that several independent sequences can be programmed at any one time, and if need be, can be linked together to provide longer sequence lengths. The digital sequencer is capable of storing many more notes than its analogue brother; often, over one thousand notes can be programmed into the memory banks. However, the sequences are generally only of one level – that is, there's only one control voltage channel output, so the device is used primarily for controlling the oscillators, and hence, the pitch.

Figure 61 shows the control panel of a typical digital sequencer, though it must be remembered that this is just a basis for describing the workings of a digital sequencer, and different models will function in slightly different manners. The Record button tells the sequencer to get ready to accept a sequence. When pressed, the Memory Indicator should reset to zero and the device will start recording as soon as the first note of the sequence is played. Some digital sequencers offer an audible metronome facility as an aid when recording a sequence. You'll be surprised how difficult it is to get the timing exactly right when simultaneously operating the sequencer.

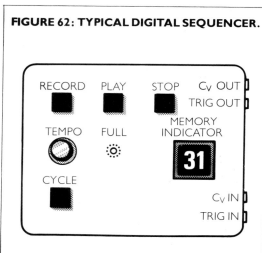

FIGURE 62: TYPICAL DIGITAL SEQUENCER.

Figure 62 illustrates the way in which the digital sequencer is hooked up to the synthesizer. Unlike the analogue sequencer, it is vital that the same voltage/frequency ratio is common to both devices. For instance, if the synthesizer operates on a one volt per octave principle, a linear sequencer cannot be used. Today, most digital sequencers adhere to this relationship, however.

From the diagram, it is clear that the synthesizer must have Control Voltage in and out, and Trigger/Gate in and out sockets. If these are not available, most synthesizers can be modified to incorporate such access points. Once the sequencer has been hooked up via the four leads (three if the synthesizer/sequencer arrangement uses switch triggers), then the sequence has to be loaded into the sequencer. The unit is simply switched into record mode, and the sequence played on the keyboard (or whatever control medium is being used); the memory indicator will unnervingly count out every note played. When approaching the end of the sequence, you should be ready with your left hand (or footswitch) to activate the Stop button. Unless you tell the sequencer how long the last note has to sound, it will automatically be given the maximum seven seconds' value – so the sequencer has to be stopped as the first beat of the next bar sounds. This is most easily accomplished by tapping one's foot in time with the sequence and hitting the Stop button just as the next bar starts, *on* the beat. This procedure is the most tricky consideration when operating a digital sequencer – so it isn't that difficult to use!

To replay the sequence, simply press the Play button (or equivalent); the sequencer will then run either as a "one-shot" whence it will just play the sequence through once, or the pattern can be continuously repeated by activating the Cycle switch.

The advantages of the digital sequencer over the simple tape recorder are considerable. For a start, once the information is fed into the sequencer, the pitch, timbre, shape and tempo of the sequence can be modified. By varying the Tempo control, the pattern can be sped up or slowed down without changing the pitch of the sequence. This enables complex patterns to be played at break-neck speed exactly as required.

The sequence can be transposed into any other key, either by using the control voltage from the synthesizer, or by means of the transposition controls on many digital sequencers. The whole character of a sequence can be transformed by adjusting the envelope controls of the synthesizer voice module during playback. But, note that, if the attack time of the voltage controlled amplifier envelope is too great, then the note won't get a chance to sound. Best effects are obtained by having envelopes with fast attack times, and taking down the sustain and decay/release controls.

Many people don't realize that you can't play *along* with a sequencer on the synthesizer if it is a monophonic model. If you think about it, it's obvious, as the sequencer is using the synthesizer's voice module. It is therefore necessary, if you want to play along with your sequence to use either a synthesizer with more than one voice module, or another instrument, or to record the played-back sequence on a tape recorder, and then to play along with the recording.

THE POLYPHONIC SEQUENCER

The polyphonic sequencer is a device that enables the player to record more than one layer of sequence. Obviously, each layer has to have its own voice module, although a series of monophonic synthesizers could be used as opposed to a polyphonic instrument. There are two distinct types of polyphonic sequencer corresponding to the aforementioned analogue and digital devices. However, such is the complexity of the circuitry involved that all polyphonic sequencers are microprocessor-based.

The "analogue" variant operates by writing, in coded form, the sequence into the device. Each note is given a pitch (voltage) and a duration (gate); then, the time lapse before the next note has to sound has to be specified. This has to be done for each layer (voice module), so it can take quite a time to program in a complete piece of music. The best known examples of this type of device are the **Roland MC-8** and the more recent **MC-4**. Remember, with this type of sequencer, the information flow is player to sequencer to synthesizer(s).

The digital polyphonic sequencer functions, as does its monophonic namesake, with the information flowing from player to keyboard to sequencer and back to synthesizer during replay. The only digital polyphonic sequencers available are specially designed to operate with certain machines; as yet, there is no universal digital interfacing system that can be adopted. However, it seems likely that this state of affairs will be remedied in the not too distant future.

ACTIVE FOOTPEDALS

An active device is one that actually does or produces something. In this case, an active footpedal produces control voltages that can be used to modify or modulate any of the voltage controllable parameters. A footpedal can, therefore, be used to pitchbend notes, or to introduce modulation; some pedals actually incorporate a low frequency oscillator, or act simply as a volume control. It is an especially helpful device when used in conjunction with a polyphonic synthesizer, as both hands are normally pretty well occupied on the keyboard and control panel.

SPATIAL EFFECT UNITS

The sound produced by most electronic musical instruments is very "dry" and dead. This is because these instruments are generating purely electronic signals; they haven't had any contact with the acoustic medium before being amplified through a loudspeaker. In order to inject some atmosphere into this dead sound, various spatial effect generators can be utilized.

REVERBERATION

This is the effect that we associate with bathrooms, churches and similar places, whereby a sound is bounced off various hard surfaces causing a reinforcement to the initial sound. When an instrument, (say a church organ), produces a sound in a highly reverberative environment, the sound bounces off all the walls, floor and ceiling, causing a series of multiple echoes. Now, the ear can only detect separate sounds that occur less than one tenth of a second apart, so these multiple echoes tend to run into one another, causing a sustaining effect to the organ playing.

Reverberation can be simulated electronically, using a series of multiple delay lines, each delaying the signal a different length of time, thus causing a simulated reverberation. Alternatively, and more commonly, a reverb spring is used. The sound which is to be processed is fed into a transducer which is connected to a metal spring, or sometimes a large metal plate; the signal causes the transducer to set up vibrations in the spring which are, in turn, picked up by another transducer at the other end of the spring, where the signal is reconstructed. The spring has, however, introduced a complex series of reflections to the vibrations travelling down its length, such that the processed signal exhibits the required reverberative effect.

Reverberation is a particularly useful tool when imitating existing acoustic instruments, as just a hint of this effect tends to bring the simulated voicing alive.

ECHO

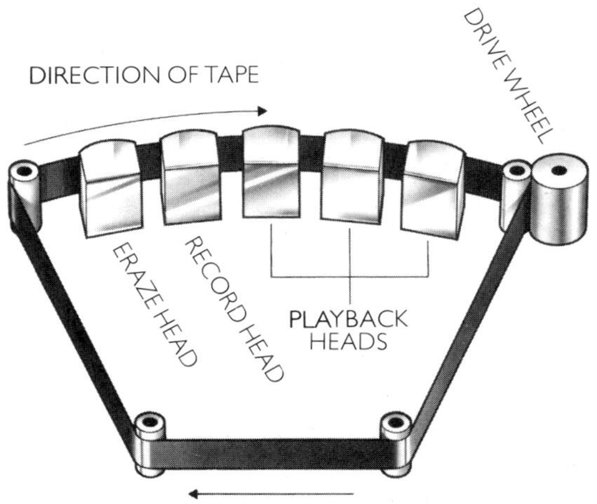

Echoes are produced when sound waves strike a hard, smooth object and are bounced back to their source. For example, if you stand at the bottom of a canyon and shout or clap your hands, the sound will be reflected off the rock face back towards you. Depending on the distance you are from the reflecting surface, the greater, (or lesser), will be the time between the production of the sound and the reception of the reflected one. This effect is put to use in submarines, and ships – a signal is sent down to the bottom of the sea, and the time taken for the reflected wave to return is measured; this time can then be used to calculate the depth of water.

FIGURE 63 : TAPE ECHO MECHANISM.

In electronic music, a glorified tape recorder is used to produce the effect of echo. The signal is recorded onto a piece of tape at one point, then taken off at another; the echo time is therefore dependent on the speed at which the tape travels between the two heads, and on the distance between them **(see figure 63).** An echo consists of a series of *distinct* repeats as opposed to the multiple reflections that cause reverberation.

THE CHORUS UNIT

This is a device that slightly changes the pitch of the incoming signal and then reconstitutes it with the original. The effect is rather like that of using the two oscillators slightly out of tune with one another, and the dimension and depth of the sound quality is enhanced considerably, so that a solo violin-like sound would fatten out to become more like a string section.

THE PHASING UNIT

A similar device to the chorus unit although the effect produced is somewhat less natural. A phaser causes the phase angle of the sound to vary at a definable rate, causing a "whooshing-"like dimension to be added to the sound. This effect is particularly suited to full range signals, and in particular for processing white noise-based voices.

6
A HISTORY

The first instrument that can, on reflection, be classified as a synthesizer was built between 1896 and 1906 by Thaddeus Cahill. The instrument was known as the **Telharmonium,** and certainly was a very impressive instrument. In fact it weighed 200 tons! This weight included the loudspeakers, but, even so, the Telharmonium was several thousand times heavier than the equivalent instruments of today. In order to move this monstrosity across America, six railway trucks were required.

The Telharmonium was a polyphonic instrument with a touch sensitive keyboard; the oscillators consisted of a series of rapidly spinning alternators driven by banks of electric motors and producing alternating currents as the required fixed frequencies. So great was the noise produced by the mechanics of the instrument that it had to be housed in a different room to the speakers, so that the noise of the motors didn't drown out the music. It also needed two people to "play" the Telharmonium. Consequently, it was, to say the least, a tricky operation to render even the simplest of pieces!

Since the Telharmonium wasn't the most portable of musical instruments, a scheme was dreamed up to sell the music it produced by transmitting it on telegraph wires to the general public. Unfortunately, this project never got off the ground, which is something of a pity as it would have constituted the first example of cable entertainment.

In 1904, Fleming invented the radio valve (or diode), which unfortunately rendered most of Cahill's concepts completely out of date. Soon, a device known as the audion, a variant of the radio valve, enabled electronic amplifiers and modulators to be built. Then came the triode, a device that was really to set the communication world on its head.

The progress in the understanding of electricity was accelerating rapidly, although its application to the musical instrument industry was remarkably slow. It wasn't until 1924 when a young Leon Theremin developed an instrument known as the **Aetherophone**, that the world was made aware of the possibilities of electricity in the musical instrument sphere. Theremin's revolutionary instrument, soon to have its name changed to that of its inventor, was a runaway success. Instead of a keyboard, two antennae were mounted on top of the main body of the instrument; one governed the pitch of the note, the other the loudness. The **Theremin** was played by moving one's hands towards and away from the antennae, to control the pitch and amplitude of each note. The instrument used two very high frequency oscillators (well above the audio spectrum); one of these was fixed, whilst the pitch of the other responded to the proximity of the players hand. The actual note heard was produced as a beat frequency set up by the interaction of the other two oscillators (see Chapter 2.).

The Theremin was a monophonic instrument, with both pitch and amplitude fully variable by the player; there was, however, little control over the timbre. The Theremin enjoyed a very long life, as it was available right up into the Sixties. (Incidentally, Dr Robert Moog, the man responsible for a lot of the major synthesizer developments, used to sell Theremin kits whilst at college, in order to finance his studies). Probably the best known example of the sound produced by the Theremin can be heard on The Beach Boys recording of "Good Vibrations."

Following on from the Theremin came a French descendant – the **Ondes Musicales,** later to be known as the **Ondes Martenot.** The player wore a ring on his finger and the position of the ring controlled the pitch of the note. A degree of control over the timbre was possible with the Ondes Musicales and several famous (French) composers, notably Dutilleux, Honnegger, and Messiaen wrote for the instrument. It retained its popularity for a considerable time, finding its way onto many American recordings of the 1950's and onto television and radio commercials of that period.

In Germany, a country renowned for its advances in electronic music, an inventor by the name of Frederich Trautwein developed the **Trautonium** in 1930. This instrument utilized a piece of wire stretched above a metal rail; by pressing the wire against the rail at the correct place, an electrical circuit was produced, causing a neon tube, or valve, to oscillate at a specific frequency. This system was similar to the Moog ribbon controller which was to appear some forty years later. The volume of the note produced was controlled by a foot-pedal, and, with the aid of harmonic filters, various tone colours could be built up. Originally, Trautwein's instrument was a monophonic device, but it was later redesigned as the **Mixtur-Trautonium,** with two sets of generators enabling the performer to produce two notes simultaneously. Such notable composers as Richard Strauss and Hindemith have scored parts for the Trautonium in their works.

Laurens Hammond must have done more than any other man to get the electronic/ electric keyboard accepted by the public at large. The **Hammond** tone wheel organ, al-though not strictly a synthesizer, was one of the most important musical developments of this century. Originally, each organ used a series of tone wheels to generate the character-istic lively sound. There were ninety-one electromagnetic disc generators in each instru-ment, and these were driven by a single synchronous motor. The tone wheels were shaped so that they produced sinusoidal currents (pure fundamental tones) which could be built up into complex voicings by means of the now famous harmonic drawbar system. The Hammond organ can be considered a forerunner to the additive synthesizer.

Two other instruments came out of the Hammond factory in Chicago: the **Novachord** and the **Solovox.** The Novachord was the first major instrument to use a series of top octave tone generators, which were subsequently divided to provide the pitches required for the entire range of the instrument. This system was employed by many organ manufacturers as an alternative to electro-mechanical tone generation, requiring as it did a separate gen-erator for each note. The Novachord was less of an organ, however, and more an ancestor to today's polyphonic synthesizers.

The Solovox was a small instrument with a two-and-a-half octave monophonic key-board. It was designed to fit just under the right hand side of a piano's keyboard, and served as an alternate sound source on which to play the melody or solo line. A series of switches just below the keyboard enabled the player to vary the pitch and timbre of the output.

Many inventors beavered away in small garage workshops while others received large sums of money from educational establishments. All were devizing various methods of combining electronics and music. A common line of development centred around the paper tape reader. At the Paris Exposition of 1929, Messrs. Couplet and Givelet introduced their "Automatically operating musical instrument of the electric oscillation type." This used a paper tape reader to control a set of four voices in much the same way that a pianola or player piano operated. But, not only were the *notes* dictated by the tape, but also the

SEQUENTIAL CIRCUITS
PROPHET X

ROLAND PROMARS COMPUPHONIC

YAMAHA C5 15D PRESET SYNTHESIZER

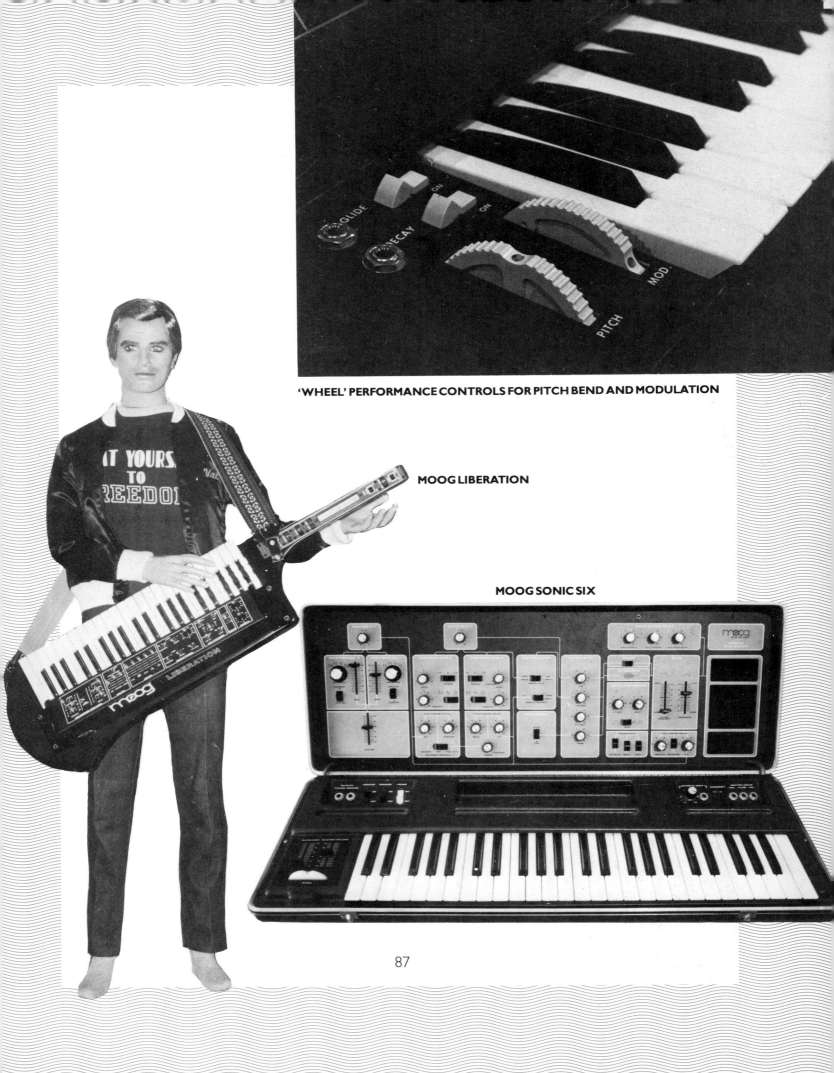

'WHEEL' PERFORMANCE CONTROLS FOR PITCH BEND AND MODULATION

MOOG LIBERATION

MOOG SONIC SIX

87

amplitude, articulation, modulation and timbre for each voice – in fact, all the parameters that a synthesizer shapes when producing a sound. Although this instrument didn't take off commercially, it set the ball rolling for other information storage machines such as the *Kent Music Box* of the early Fifties, and more importantly, the *RCA Music Synthesizer.*

The RCA Music Synthesizer was the machine that really showed the world what was possible with the electronic technology of the day. Designed initially by Dr. Harry F. Olson, and Herbert Belar in 1954, it was later redesigned as the *RCA Mk II,* and installed in the Columbia-Princetown studio in New York. The instrument used a two keyboard system to produce perforated tape instructions for defining the synthesizer's main parameters. When these tapes were fed into the instrument, they were automatically synchronized with two master disc recorders, each of which had six recording channels. The sixteen-inch discs could each handle a six-channel recording of up to three minutes. This would then be mixed down to a single track and transferred to the second recorder and the process could be repeated until the second recorder was full – a 36-track capacity (6 × 6). If necessary, these tracks could then be mixed back onto the original recorder, and more tracks added.

The actual voice production side of the RCA machine was monophonic, so this multi-channel disc system was integral to the operation of the synthesizer. All the voice circuitry utilized valves, so to have built a polyphonic RCA machine would have been a gargantuan task. As it was, the instrument cost £60,000 – at 1955 prices! The RCA Music Synthesizer was very much in demand during the late '50s and '60s and was the last link in the chain before the advent of the voltage controlled synthesizer.

In 1963, Herb Deutsch, an electronic composer and instructor at Hofstra University, met up with Robert Moog at a conference in Rochester, New York. Moog had been in-terested in electronics since his childhood, and whilst at college, he had marketed Theremin kits. They discussed the possibility of developing a small solid state instrument that would offer some of the facilities of the RCA Music Synthesizer to the smaller recording studios. Deutsch and Moog worked together throughout the summer of 1964 on the basis of using voltage to define the various elements of a sound (pitch, timbre, and loudness).

They succeeded, and by the end of the year, Moog had built a prototype instrument which Deutsch revealed to the world at the AES Convention. During 1965, production facilities were set up to manufacture Moog's electronic music modules, which, at that time, were made entirely by hand. Moog's devices became increasingly sought after, but it wasn't until Walter (now Wendy) Carlos recorded an album called *Switched on Bach* which spot-lighted one of Moog's modular systems, that things really started to happen. The album was to become the biggest selling "classical" record of all time, and Moog's electronic synthe-sizers were established.

Demand grew for a small, performance-orientated instrument, so Moog (with the aid of designer Jim Scott) produced the *Minimoog* for the 1971 AES Convention. The Mini-moog's success, which was to last ten years, was a result of it being a true musical instrument that musicians could get to grips with, and not just a box of electronic circuitry.

During the late '60s, other designers and manufacturers were tackling the problem of producing a voltage controlled synthesizer. In Britain, Peter Zinovieff and his team at EMS were working on what was to become the *VCS 3,* an extremely versatile and popular instrument. Unfortunately, EMS lacked the business flair that would have kept them up as a world leader. Alan R. Pearlman, a businessman, engineer and keen musician sold his successful industrial electronics firm in order to concentrate on musical electronics. He had similar ideas to Moog, in that he wanted to turn the inventions of engineers into instruments that could be played by musicians who didn't possess electronics degrees. In May, 1970, he completed a large modular instrument that was known as the **ARP 2500.** Just as Moog introduced the Minimoog, ARP came out with the **2600,** which was to become one of the most popular instruments of the '70s, along with ARP's next machine, the **Odyssey.**

These instruments differ little from the majority of today's monophonic synthesizers, save that the tuning of the more recent machines is a lot steadier, and the units are generally more reliable.

The next hurdle was that of polyphony, and it wasn't until the mid-Seventies that such instruments started to appear. At first, these instruments were really just glorified organs. However, the **Polymoog,** although using master tone generators to derive the pitch of each note, did have separate filters and envelope generators for each key. At the same time, Yamaha, Oberheim and Sequential Circuits were developing their polyphonic instruments: the **CS 80, Oberheim 4-** and **8- Voice,** and the **Prophet 5** (respectively). These machines were all voice assignables with the number of synthesizer voice modules determining how many notes could be played at any one time. In fact, the Yamaha CS 80 features a layering system where two voice modules were assigned to each note – each having a different sound.

The latest advances are coming with micro computer-based systems using additive and digital synthesis. At present, most of these machines are very expensive – but we've only seen the tip of the iceberg, especially if you consider the rate at which the industry has moved during the last 25 years. There is also a trend towards low-cost polyphonic ensemble keyboards, which are destined to do to the home organ market what home organs did to piano sales. Casio, the watch and calculator people, are at the forefront of these latest products. They have developed a system of voice generation known as the "Consonance/Vowel" method. This divides a sound into two parts, with the attack (consonance) phase and the body (vowel) phase separately produced and combined to give extremely realistic simulations of existing instruments. It would seem that the future is going to lie with companies like Casio and Yamaha, who can produce instruments of outstanding performance at a cost not dreamed of ten years ago.

VANGELIS: With the *Yamaha CS80*. Also in photo. *Korg Poly Ensemble*, *ARP Pro-soloist*, *Farfisa Syntorchestra*, *Clavinet D6* and *Fender Rhodes 88*

RICK WAKEMAN: With *Korg PS3200*, *Korg BX-3*, *Korg Lambda* and *Yamaha CP80*

PETE BANKS: *Moog Multimoog*, *Roland SA 09* and *Yamaha CS80*

HERBIE HANCOCK: Playing the *Clavitar*

7
APPENDIX

RECENT DEVELOPMENTS

The world of electronic music is a particularly fast moving one. The synthesizer has been with us for less than two decades and during that period, it has completely changed the sound of popular, and to a lesser extent more serious, forms of music. The advances in electronic technology over this period have been a contributory factor in the design and, more important, the cost of electronic musical instruments. Such has been the acceleration of microprocessor applications that the computer industry has been blessed with massive capital investment. In turn, this has led to the wider availability of the microprocessor to design engineers, as this remarkable device is far cheaper to use than the discrete components it now replaces.

In a synthesizer, we have come to accept the idea that sound is created from analogue circuitry, and that the microprocessor, being a digital device, is best used as a master control system that sorts out all the instructions and commands being sent to the analogue circuitry by us, the players, through the keyboard and main control panel. Remember that analogue systems use continually varying signals (voltages), whereas a digital device operates using numbers that are made up from a series of signals that can exist only in one of two states "on" or "off" (high or low). See **figure 64.** In Chapter 3, COMPUTER BASED SYSTEMS, we learned how the computer can be used in two ways to take a more active role in the actual voice production side of synthesis. These methods are additive and direct synthesis.

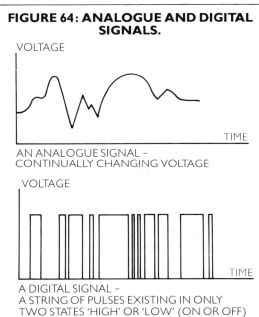

FIGURE 64: ANALOGUE AND DIGITAL SIGNALS.

VOLTAGE

TIME

AN ANALOGUE SIGNAL –
CONTINUALLY CHANGING VOLTAGE

VOLTAGE

TIME

A DIGITAL SIGNAL –
A STRING OF PULSES EXISTING IN ONLY
TWO STATES 'HIGH' OR 'LOW' (ON OR OFF)

Until recently, the cost of using the computer, or microprocessor, for such means of synthesis has been somewhat prohibitive. However, not only have prices for these devices come tumbling down, but also their performance has improved considerably. It is necessary, for reasons that we won't go into just yet, for the central processing unit (CPU) of a direct synthesis machine to operate at very high frequencies; technology is only just providing us with these high speed devices at reasonable cost and reliability.

The microprocessor, as did the integrated circuit and the transistor before it, is set to change the face, not just of the electronic music industry, but of the entire electronic and data processing world. Many advances have been made in the brief period since *The Complete Synthesizer* was first published; it is for this reason that this Appendix has been added.

REPLAY KEYBOARDS

One of the most exciting areas of development in recent times has been the use of digital synthesizing techniques in replay instruments. One of the earliest forms of replay keyboard was the **Mellotron**. This evolved from an earlier prototype device known as the **Chambelain,** but it was the Mellotron, later to become the **Novatron** (for legal reasons), that was the first commercially successful replay keyboard. At the time, it was the only real alternative to the electric/electronic organ and piano.

NOVATRON

The Mellotron/Novatron could be considered as a series of tape recorders, operating in playback mode only – hence "replay" keyboards. There would be a separate tape head and tape for each note and these were arranged so that when the associated key was played, the tape would be drawn over the tape head, and the sounds that had been pre-recorded on to the tape were "picked-up" and transduced into an audio signal. All manner of different tapes were available – from sound effects, through to symphony orchestras – and the Mellotron was essentially the forerunner of today's polyphonic string synths and preset synths.

The Mellotron, for all its remarkable qualities, suffered from several major problems: it was big and bulky, unreliable, noisy (tape hiss), and was limited to notes of around seven seconds. It was also quite a tricky job to change tapes. Despite these problems, many major bands (including The Moody Blues, Rick Wakeman and King Crimson) toured with these instruments, which provided a unique and powerful timbral backdrop. For many years, an electronic alternative to the Mellotron was sought, but there was a major problem – the amount of information stored on that seven second piece of tape, in terms of electronic memory capacity, was phenomenal. Consider **figure 65,** which shows just a fraction of a second's worth of a sound; let's look at how this may be represented in the form of digital information.

To express an analogue signal (which is what we have here) in digital terms, it is necessary to break it down into lots of little pieces. As our ears can detect frequencies of up to almost 20,000 Hz (cycles per second, see p12), in order to accurately turn this signal into digital form, it must be sampled at twice the maximum audible frequency. (The reasons for this are beyond the scope of this book.) Therefore, we have to divide one second's worth of sound into 40,000 steps, and for each step generate a number that is proportional to the value of the analogue signal at that instant. As you are aware, digital systems use binary numbers ("on" and "off"); thus, to be able to express accurately the level of the signal at this given instant, we need to use at least eight binary numbers (giving us 256 possible signal levels, and even this can be inadequate for some purposes). Now you can see that our one second piece of recording tape can handle the digital equivalent of 40,000 × 8 binary numbers. A binary digit is known as a "bit", and a string of eight a "byte". For just seven seconds, then, we need 280,000 bytes of memory!

You can now see why the electronic Mellotron isn't a particularly viable project. However, by using a microprocessor to cheat a bit, several manufacturers have developed sophisticated replay instruments that are financially accessible. The secret of the system relies on the use of digital loops. You may have experimented with tape loops, whereby you can record a sound on to a piece of magnetic tape, then edit the end of the tape to the beginning so that you have a continuous loop which can then be rigged up using pencil rollers and other such Heath Robinson devices so that the sound repeats itself. Now, a similar thing can be done digitally, only it is a lot simpler to execute.

Take **figure 66** as an example; here we have a representation of a bowed violin note – just the loudness contour is shown for the sake of simplicity. There are three distinct phases: the attack, the sustain – whence the note is remaining fairly constant – and the release phase, which takes into account the resonance of both the instrument's body and, if applicable, the local environment (i.e. reverb). Generally speaking, the attack and release phases are fairly short, say one third and two thirds of a second respectively; it is the main sustained portion of the note that takes up most of the time available. On many occasions, as with our violin example, the sound being produced during this phase is fairly constant (ignoring vibrato, or other forms of modulation), so we could take just a small portion of this part and repeat it over and over to give the impression of a fully sustained voicing. In this way, we use very little memory and can make the note sound for as long as is necessary. So, as we can see from **figure 66,** by using just one-and-a-half seconds worth of memory (a mere 60,000, or 60k bytes), we've made a pretty good

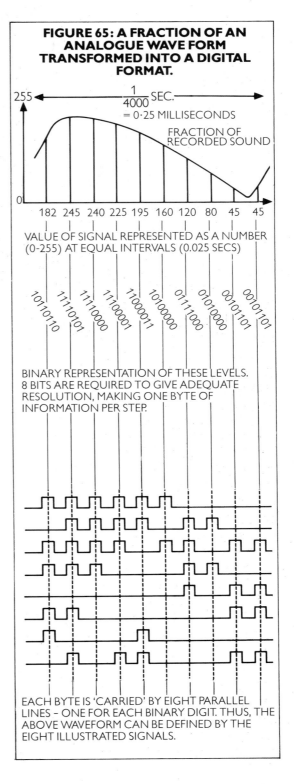

FIGURE 65: A FRACTION OF AN ANALOGUE WAVE FORM TRANSFORMED INTO A DIGITAL FORMAT.

$\frac{1}{4000}$ SEC. = 0.25 MILLISECONDS

FRACTION OF RECORDED SOUND

182 245 240 225 195 160 120 80 45 45

VALUE OF SIGNAL REPRESENTED AS A NUMBER (0-255) AT EQUAL INTERVALS (0.025 SECS)

10110110
11110101
11110000
11100001
11000011
10100000
01111000
01010000
00101101
00101101

BINARY REPRESENTATION OF THESE LEVELS. 8 BITS ARE REQUIRED TO GIVE ADEQUATE RESOLUTION, MAKING ONE BYTE OF INFORMATION PER STEP.

EACH BYTE IS 'CARRIED' BY EIGHT PARALLEL LINES - ONE FOR EACH BINARY DIGIT. THUS, THE ABOVE WAVEFORM CAN BE DEFINED BY THE EIGHT ILLUSTRATED SIGNALS.

simulation of the original sound source.

A replay synthesizer generally operates in both record and playback modes, although some instruments are designed to generate factory presets only. One of the most popular of this new generation of instruments is the **Emulator,** (see photograph), made by the Californian company E-mu Inc. This unit accepts signals of up to two seconds from an external source, which can be either a microphone or line signal. It will then transpose this sound across the entire four octave keyboard such that it presents the player with an eight voice polyphonic capability to reproduce this sampled sound. One problem that can occur when a whole chromatic spectrum of pitches is generated from a single sampled signal is that the

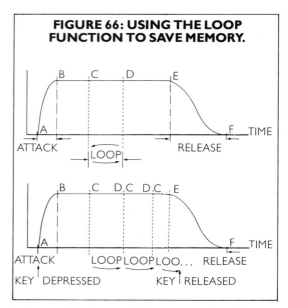

FIGURE 66: USING THE LOOP FUNCTION TO SAVE MEMORY.

inherent qualities of the sound are also transposed along with the pitch. For example, if Singer A were to render a "Hallelujah" pitched at middle C, and a note one-and-a-half octaves higher was then played, then not only would the pitch be raised, but so would the resonant frequency of the singer's voice, which would mean that it wouldn't sound the same as if singer A were to render that note directly. In order to alleviate this problem, it is necessary to sample the signal at various intervals to ensure as faithful a rendition to the original source as possible.

The Emulator is fitted with a floppy disc unit, which means that it is possible to load in pre-sampled sounds in a matter of seconds; similarly, the player can assemble his own selection of recorded sounds.

This system opens up a whole new dimension to the synthesist, who can introduce almost any form of sonic effect or simulation into his repertoire. This form of instrument may still be beyond the reaches of most musicians, for even now they are still quite a major investment. But as technology

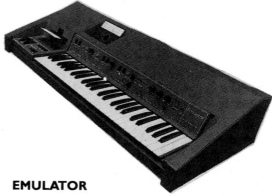

EMULATOR

brings us even cheaper memories and control circuitry, the price – like that of the synthesizer itself – will fall, making such instruments more widely available.

One problem associated with these forms of musical instrument lies not with the technical or musical side, but on the ethical side. A replay keyboard can reproduce such accurate acoustic voicings that in the recording world, acoustic musicians are starting to be replaced by these "more manageable" and versatile instruments. Why should a producer pay eight string players when he can manage with just one replay keyboard player? This is already a major discussion topic with the national musicians' unions, and in some circles, restrictions on the use of these devices are being drawn up. Similar problems have occurred in the past with more conventional polyphonic synthesizers, but the high quality performance of instruments such as the Emulator has recently polarized the situation.

COMPUTERS AND MUSIC / MUSIC AND COMPUTERS

The electronic musical instrument industry is currently being threatened by the infiltration of the computer. We are now seeing the advent of the personal computer – a computer in every home – and this makes a very attractive base on which to build an electronic music system. Whereas we were once seeing instruments that had a micro-computer incorporated into their circuitry, we are now getting computer companies developing low-cost music packages to link up with their equipment, thus encroaching into the instrument manufacturers' territory.

But can a music system that is designed as a microcomputer "add-on" compete with a fully fledged synthesizer, that has been designed to meet the exacting requirements of today's musicians? At present the answer is a reserved "no", but in a few years time, when the computer market has evolved to the next generation, then it will pose a positive threat to the electronic musical instrument industry.

THE HOME COMPUTER AND MUSIC

The current trend is to use the home computer as a glorified sequencer. Several computer companies offer music packages, and generally these consist of a voice card, which plugs into the computer's expansion sockets (these are usually to be found inside the computer and enable various extra facilities to be added to the computer system), and some special software for controlling the music output. "Software" is the name given to the program that tells the computer what to do; it is generally programmed into the unit by means of a floppy disc, or cassette tape (in a similar fashion to the way in which programmable polyphonic synthesizers use a cassette for storing patch programs).

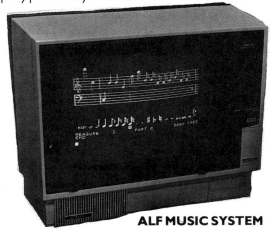

ALF MUSIC SYSTEM

One such package is made for the Apple computer, and is known as the **ALF Music System.** A voice card slots into the Apple's expansion socket, the software is loaded (via a floppy disc) into the computer, and up comes a list of various options on the monitor screen. To use an ALF Music System – or in fact most other such music packages – requires next to no computer programming knowledge; the way in which the program is formatted shows you exactly how to operate the computer and control the music output.

The voice cards usually contain the circuitry for several voices, and in the ALF's case there are nine such voices. Computer voices are quite different to the synthesizer voice modules we looked at in chapter 2. Generally, computer voices are based on the square wave, which isn't suprising as the computer operates entirely by sending pulse and square waves back and forth. **Figure 67** shows a typical computer voice of the type to be found in low cost packages such as the ALF. The "oscillator" consists of the basic square wave, which, on some systems, may be reshaped to provide other waveforms; the source signal is then fed through the equivalent of a voltage controlled amplifier, with a digitally controlled envelope shaper.

Before "playing" the computer music system, it is first necessary to identify the actual sound you want to use. Therefore, we have to define Pitch, Waveshape (if applicable), the Loudness Contour (often this is similar to an ADSR or DADSR envelope), and overall Level. This may seem rather restricting: there's no filter or filter envelope, and little or no timbral control. However, things aren't as bad as they may seem, because it is possible to introduce more complex timbres by paralleling voices, and to vary the timbral

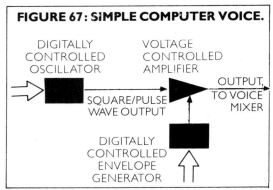

FIGURE 67: SIMPLE COMPUTER VOICE.

DIGITALLY CONTROLLED OSCILLATOR

VOLTAGE CONTROLLED AMPLIFIER

SQUARE/PULSE WAVE OUTPUT

OUTPUT, TO VOICE MIXER

DIGITALLY CONTROLLED ENVELOPE GENERATOR

to that of the additive synthesizer (p64). This will be dealt with in more depth shortly.

Different systems are employed by the various design companies for programming actual musical scores into the computer. On these lower priced packages there is, of course, no music keyboard to play, so the information is either fed in using the computer's alpha-numeric keyboard or by utilizing the games paddles (which usually take the form of control knobs or joysticks, and are a good way of feeding analogue information into a computer).

The ALF system is a particularly simple method: the computer draws out a musical stave, the operator identifies the time signature and key, then loads the actual notes one by one by positioning a cursor (a flashing dot) on the required line or space of the stave, and selecting the value of the note using a second cursor (both cursors being moved by the two games paddles). In this way, the computer actually writes out the music as it is

RHODES CHROMA

programmed. When one melody line has been completed, the computer returns to the start and a new voice is selected, a new sound defined, and the second line of music programmed, and so on. When the complete composition has been loaded into the computer, it can be stored on a second floppy disc for use at a later date. It can be seen that this type of system is, in effect, a form of advanced sequencing, and that the instrument cannot be played in real time – i.e. you cannot just walk up to the computer, switch it on, and play a tune; the tune has first to be programmed into the computer, either by the user, or from a pre-loaded floppy disc.

ADVANCED MICROCOMPUTER MUSIC SYSTEMS.

The demand for music packages for use with home computers and microcomputers has been growing rapidly. Several "software houses" (companies who write computer programmes to run on various computer systems) have developed larger and more versatile music software and hardware (the actual circuitry that makes up a system) to make the computer more of a musical instrument, and thus more accessible to the player. The first pre-requisite for such a set-up is a real time controller so that the "instrument" can be played in the normal fashion. The music keyboard is the obvious controller, and several systems that consist of keyboard, voice cards, and software are now available.

ALPHASYNTAURI

As well as featuring a keyboard, to get the most out of such a configuration necessitates the use of a more versatile voice card than that of the ALF. The prime voice card system currently available is manufactured by Mountain Computer Inc., and is, once again, designed for operation with the Apple computer. Although the voice card is made by one company, several of the software houses have developed various systems for using this voice card to maximum effect. One such company is the Syntauri Corporation, who market a product known as the **alphaSyntauri** which uses the Mountain voice card, a 61-note dynamic keyboard, and their own comprehensive software.

The advanced voice cards used by such systems differ from the more basic square-wave voices in that the actual oscillator waveforms can be uniquely described. This can be done either by (1) specifying the amplitudes of each of the harmonics – additive synthesis (p64); or (2) breaking the waveform down into tiny steps (in the alphaSyntauri's case 256 steps) and giving each step a value – a form of direct synthesis (p66 **figure 55**). When the waveform has been constructed, the loudness contour can be defined using a fairly standard envelope system. The ability to control the exact harmonic content (i.e. the shape of the waveform) makes this a very versatile set-up. Once you have defined the desired voicings, you can then set about combining voices to further expand the instrument's synthesizing capabilities.

WAVEFORM MANIPULATION

The main problem with the computer based systems so far described is that they have no form of filter as in the analogue subtractive instruments. It would appear, therefore, that there is no way to vary the timbre with time (as described on p43). There is, however, a simple solution to this problem; this involves the combination of signals from two or more voices.

As an example, let's take the simulation of an electronic organ voicing. There are two distinct phases to consider – the percussive attack part of the note, and the main body. **Figure 68** shows how this can be simulated by using both a basic subtractive synthesizer (with a standard synthesizer voice module) and a computer based system.

The subtractive synthesizer uses VCO 1 as the harmonic percussion pitch, and VCO 2 as the main body of the sound. When a note is played, the filter envelope is triggered such that it opens fully then quickly closes down, removing most of VCO 1's higher frequencies, and leaving VCO 2 to act as the dominant sound source. The computer voices, having no filter, have to be used slightly differently. One voice is set at the percussion pitch with a percussive envelope, whilst the second acts as the main body of the note. The outputs from the two voices are then layered on top of one another, thus providing the organ simulation.

By manipulating and layering the computer's voices, it is possible to simulate the variation of timbre with time, but unfortunately this isn't nearly as satisfactory as the subtractive filtering system. Nevertheless, the ability of the more advanced systems to accurately construct the oscillator waveforms is an extremely positive benefit.

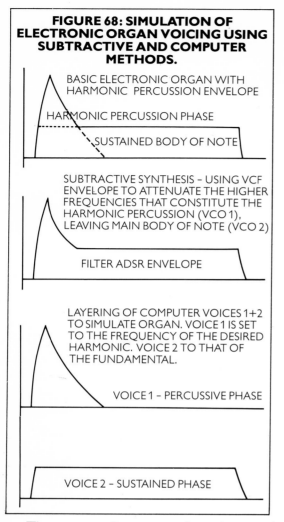

FIGURE 68: SIMULATION OF ELECTRONIC ORGAN VOICING USING SUBTRACTIVE AND COMPUTER METHODS.

BASIC ELECTRONIC ORGAN WITH HARMONIC PERCUSSION ENVELOPE

HARMONIC PERCUSSION PHASE

SUSTAINED BODY OF NOTE

SUBTRACTIVE SYNTHESIS – USING VCF ENVELOPE TO ATTENUATE THE HIGHER FREQUENCIES THAT CONSTITUTE THE HARMONIC PERCUSSION (VCO 1), LEAVING MAIN BODY OF NOTE (VCO 2)

FILTER ADSR ENVELOPE

LAYERING OF COMPUTER VOICES 1+2 TO SIMULATE ORGAN. VOICE 1 IS SET TO THE FREQUENCY OF THE DESIRED HARMONIC. VOICE 2 TO THAT OF THE FUNDAMENTAL.

VOICE 1 – PERCUSSIVE PHASE

VOICE 2 – SUSTAINED PHASE

COMPUTER MUSICAL INSTRUMENTS

This final category of computer based systems enables the player to break free of the restrictions imposed by the basic waveform manipulation required by the preceding configurations. Essentially, these instruments are capable of having the output waveforms of each voice accurately defined at each instant in time. Therefore, it follows that accurate programming of periodic and aperiodic variation of timbre with time is possible.

This programming of the sounds into these instruments can be a laborious operation if you specify the various individual waveforms that are to be "merged" into a single voicing, so various aids are employed to speed things up. Light-pens can be used to "draw" the waveforms directly on to the computer's visual display unit (monitor screen), or additive synthesis methods can be employed (see p64). Sampling is also possible, whereby an external sound source can be fed into the instrument, analysed by the computer, then recreated using the voice cards (see **Replay Keyboards**). One of the good things about this approach is that the computer analysis of the source signal is depicted on the computer's screen, so you can see exactly how a particular sound is formed.

The power of computer based musical instruments is unmatched by any other form of electronic synthesizer. However, this fact is most certainly reflected in the cost of such products, which puts them beyond the reach of all but the most affluent of musicians. The main markets for these instruments are top-line recording studios, music colleges and universities.

THE SYNTHESIZER AND THE COMPUTER

Synthesizer manufacturers are aware that computers are moving in on their territory and, as a result, are seeking to facilitate the use of the computer with their products. Many synthesizers, both monophonic and polyphonic, are now provided with some form of computer interface to enable the player to link his instrument up to a small microcomputer.

This development is a logical one; it is also beneficial to the player. In most cases, the computer can be used to do the job of a sequencer, although some companies have designed their interface system so that elementary program manipulation can also be achieved, and this opens up a much wider area of control. The computer most definitely has a major role to play in the design of future instruments, and although there will always be a demand for a simple preset instrument, the increasingly technical minds of today's musicians will ensure that tomorrow's instruments utilize to the full, the advances that science will bring us.

THE GLOSSARY

Additive Synthesis: The construction of more complex tones from a series of fundamental frequencies (i.e. sine waves). This synthesis technique relies on the principle that any periodic waveshape can be constructed by adding together sine waves of varying amplitudes and frequencies.

ADSR: An abbreviation of Attack, Decay, Sustain, Release – the four prime parameters to be found as part of an envelope generator.

Amplitude: The amount of any signal is known as its amplitude. In respect of an audio signal, the amplitude corresponds to the loudness at which we perceive the signal. In electrical terms, the amplitude is a measurement of the amount a voltage is fluctuating.

Amplitude Modulation: In a synthesizer, the amplitude of a signal can be controlled by a voltage. If this voltage is changing, then the signal is said to be experiencing amplitude modulation. The most common form of modulation is tremolo, which occurs when a sub-audio oscillation, usually in the form of a sine wave, is used to modulate the amplitude.

Analogue: A signal or voltage that is continuously variable, i.e. one that can theoretically be set at any level. An analogue device is one that responds directly to a control voltage.

Analogue/Digital Convertor: A device that will sample an analogue signal (voltage) and transform it into a digital representation of that signal. This digital code can then be subsequently processed by other digital devices.

Analogue Sequencer: A sequencer that handles continuous analogue signals. Normally, this device generates its own control signals, providing a series of control voltages and gate/trigger pulses that are set up manually on the control panel. These voltages are fed out in series to the synthesizer.

Aperiodic Waveform: An irregular, non-repeating waveform without pitch.

AR: An abbreviation of Attack Release, two control parameters to be found in a simplified envelope generator.

Assignment: A term that is applicable to polyphonic synthesizers, referring to the determination as to which voice module is to be controlled by which note currently being played.

Attack: A parameter of the envelope generator. This is the time, at the start of the envelope, that the output voltage takes to reach its peak level.

Attenuator: A device that is used to reduce the amplitude of the signal passing through it.

Azure Noise: A random signal, weighted so that the higher frequencies are more pronounced. Can be heard as a hissing sound.

Balanced Modulator: See **Ring Modulator.**

Band Pass Filter: A device that allows only those signals around a certain frequency (the cut-off frequency) to pass.

Band Reject (Notch) Filter: A device designed to allow all frequencies, other than those around a certain frequency (the cut-off frequency) to pass.

Beat: The interaction caused by two closely related pitches sounding simultaneously. This interaction takes the form of a wavering in the loudness of the total sound, and is a useful means of tuning two pitches together (eliminating the beats).

Bend: The process of smoothly sharpening or flattening the pitch of a note. The term comes from the "bending" of guitar strings to alter the pitch.

Centre Dente: A physical notch in a control mechanism (potentiometer, slider, etc.) that enables the operator to return the control to its original centre position after use. Particularly common on pitch-bend controls.

Clamping: The limitation of a voltage to a specified level.

Clock: Regular low frequency pulse waveform used for driving sequencers, control sampling, time storage of information, triggering etc.

Contour: See **Envelope**

Contour Amount: Control that determines the amount of effect the envelope generator will have over the voltage controlled parameter it is driving (normally the VCF or VCA).

Controller: A device that provides a control voltage and gate/trigger pulse in order to drive one or more synthesizer voice modules, e.g. a keyboard.

Control Voltage: A signal that is used to tell voltage controllable parameters what to do.

Cut-off Frequency: The frequency at which the filter is set to operate. This parameter is normally both voltage controllable and manually variable.

Decay: A parameter of the envelope generator, it is the rate at which the output voltage falls from its maximum level before reaching the sustain level. For ADR, the decay setting also determines the time that the output voltage takes to die away to zero after the key has been released.

Module: A device that makes up part of a modular system. See also **Voice Module.**

Monochord: An effect possible on a monophonic, multi-oscillator synthesizer. The oscillators are tuned to certain intervals, (e.g. the fundamental, third and fifth), and this fixed chord is transposed by the keyboard's (controller) control voltage.

Monophonic: A type of synthesizer capable of playing only one independent note at a time– i.e. there is only one voice module. If more than one key is played, only one note will sound. See (High, Low and Last Note) **Priority.**

Multiple: Found only on modular systems, this passive circuit enables a signal or control voltage to be split and sent off to two or more other modules.

Multiple Trigger: A triggering system employed by certain manufacturers whereby a new trigger pulse is generated every time a new key is struck, even if previously held keys haven't been released.

Negative Feedback: Occurring when part of the signal from the output of a device (e.g. an amplifier or filter) is fed back to the input, but with its polarity or phase opposite to that of the input signal. This leads to a dampening of the resulting signal.

Noise Generator: A source of random voltage fluctuations, which, when converted to an audible signal, sound like a radio that is tuned in between VHF channels.

Non-Volatile Memory: A type of memory system, that will retain the information it possesses even when the power has been switched off.

Notch Filter: See **Band Reject Filter.**

One Shot: An event that has to be re-triggered every time it is required to occur, i.e. a single event.

Oscillator: An electronic circuit that produces a constantly repeating waveform.

Overtones: The various frequency components that make up a sound. These may be of any mathematical relationship to the fundamental. See also **Harmonics.**

Patch: The way in which the various synthesizer blocks are hooked up. See **Hard-wired.**

Patch Cords/Leads: The cables that are used to hook up the various sections of a modular system.

Performance Controls: The group of controls situated close to the keyboard (controller) that are used to modify the character of the note whilst it is sounding. Normally, these control some form of pitchbender, a modulation control, a master volume, and a portamento rate control.

Periodic: A regular repeating waveform, thus exhibiting pitch.

Phase: The point in the cycle of a periodic waveform where the oscillator is, at any particular instance. Two sine waves, for example, may be of the same frequency and sound the same, but, if they started their cycles at different times, they would have a different phase relationship. The period the two waves are apart is known as the phase difference or phase angle.

Phase Locking: A circuit that detects the difference in phase between two signals and then changes the frequency of one so that they match.

Pink Noise: A random combination of all frequencies in equal amounts over each octave of the audio spectrum.

Pitch bend: See **Bend.**

Pitch to Voltage Converter: A device that measures the frequency of an incoming signal and produces a control voltage proportional to this frequency, such that, when the voltage is applied to a VCO, the pitch of the oscillator will track that of the incoming signal.

Polyphonic: The ability of a synthesizer to play more than one note simultaneously. Some keyboard synthesizers are capable of playing as many notes as there are keys; others use a voice assignment system and can play, for instance, only 4, 6, 8, or 10 voices.

Portamento: See **Glide.**

Positive Feedback: This occurs when the signal that is fed back to the device from the output has the same polarity or phase as the input. The feedback signal, therefore, tends to reinforce the input signal – often to such a degree that self-oscillation occurs.

Pre-patched: See **Hard-wired.**

Preset: A button or switch used to select a certain pre-programmed voicing. When selected, all the variable parameters of the synthesizer voice module are automatically set to produce the desired sound.

Pressure Sensitivity: A feature of certain keyboards sometimes known as second touch. It refers to the generation of an additional control voltage, the level of which is dependent on how much pressure is applied to the key after it has been depressed. This voltage can be used to bend the pitch, open the filter, increase the amplitude, etc.

Programmable: The ability to store a certain patch in a memory circuit so that the sound can be recalled and recreated at a later time.

Pulse Wave: A waveshape generated by an oscillator consisting of an alternating high and low steady state voltage.

Pulse Width: See **Duty Cycle.**

Pulse Width Modulation: The automatic variation in the pulse width or duty cycle of a pulse wave by a control signal (normally, the LFO). The resulting effect is the fattening up of the sound – comparable with the sound of two oscillators almost in unison.

Q: See **Resonance.**

Quantized: A continuously changing voltage is quantized by slotting it into specific voltage steps, i.e. the voltage can exist only as certain values. The most common form of quantizing is that of converting the voltages produced by potentiometers (control knobs) such that, when it is applied to a voltage controlled oscillator, the pitch will sweep in semitonal steps.

Ramp Wave: An oscillator output waveform that rises smoothly to a peak, then drops instantaneously to its starting point. This waveform can be either of two states: ramp up, as described above: or ramp down, the above inverted. The ramp wave has a brassy quality to it due to its relatively rich harmonic content.

Release: The envelope generator parameter that governs how long it takes for the output voltage to return to its initial position after the key (hence gate) has been released.

Resonance: This is caused by applying positive feedback around the filter, and has the effect of causing those frequencies close to the cut-off point to be emphasized to an extent that a ringing can be detected. Extreme degrees of resonance result in the filter breaking into self-oscillation.

Ribbon: A controller that puts out a voltage dependent on where along its surface it is pressed. It is most commonly used for pitchbending.

Ringing: See **Resonance.**

Ring Modulator: A device that accepts two audio signals and puts out two different signals, one consisting of the arithmetic sum of the input frequencies, the other the difference. This circuit is most often used in the production of a clangorous sound, e.g. bells and gongs etc.

Roll-off: The rate at which a signal is attenuated by a filter. Ideally, all frequencies beyond the cut-off point of a filter would be removed completely; however, this isn't the case, and the roll-off characteristic of a filter identifies the rate of attenuation of these filtered signals. The roll-off is measured in dB/octave.

Sample and Hold: A device that accepts a clock pulse, and samples a given signal on every pulse from the clock. The voltage at this instant is held in the circuit's memory until the next clock pulse samples a new level.

Sawtooth Wave: See **Ramp Wave.**

Scaling: A normal controller will double the frequency of the oscillators for every octave jump. However, some synthesizers have a variable scaling facility enabling a microtonal scaling to be set up.

Schmitt Trigger: A device that samples an incoming signal, and puts out a pulse every time that signal goes over a predetermined threshold level.

Self-Oscillation: See **Resonance.**

Sequencer: A device that produces user determined sequences of voltages, that can be cycled to produce bass patterns, melody lines, special effects etc.

Sine Wave: A smooth, continuously changing waveform that has a pure tone. It is a fundamental waveform with no overtones or harmonics.

Single Trigger: This is a system employed on certain instruments whereby a new trigger pulse is generated only when all the other keys have been released. This enables the playing of legato passages without retriggering the envelope generators.

Split Keyboard: A keyboard controller that has an electrical division such that one manual is divided into two halves, each with separate signal outputs.

Square Wave: A pulse wave with a 50 per cent duty cycle. It has a clear, hollow quality to it.

Static Filter: A filter whose characteristics remain fixed once set by the front panel controls, i.e. it isn't voltage controllable.

Sub-Audio: A frequency below the threshold of human hearing (around 16 Hz).

Subtractive Synthesis: A system of synthesis whereby the starting point is a waveform rich in harmonics, which is then processed by a series of harmonic filters in order to remove unwanted harmonics and so produce the desired sound.

Sustain: The third phase of the ADSR envelope, this is the level at which the envelope output settles down for as long as the key remains held.

Switch Trigger: A type of trigger signal that produces a shorting to ground at the outputs when activated. It is, therefore, a simple process to parallel up various such trigger sources.

Synchronization: The locking together of two oscillators at the beginning of one of their cycles.

Touch Pad/Switch: A control that has no moving parts, but is activated merely by touch. It can be used to switch any parameter that is controlled by a mechanical switch.

Touch Responsive: Generally, this refers to the type of keyboard that has no moving parts – just a series of touch pads arranged to represent conventional keys.

Touch Sensitive: Applies to a type of keyboard that can sense the speed or pressure with which a key is struck and produce a proportional control voltage.

Transient Generator: See **Envelope**

Tremolo: See **Amplitude Modulation.**

Triangle Wave: An oscillator output waveform that rises smoothly to a peak, then falls at a similar rate until it reaches its starting point whence it repeats. It has a smooth, muted tonal quality, a bit like a sine wave, though because of its harmonic content it is less pure.

Trigger: A signal produced by the controller that tells the envelope generators when to start their cycles.

Unison: When two or more oscillators are running at the same frequency.

Variable: A control parameter that is continuously variable, i.e. one that isn't just on or off, nor, strictly speaking, quantized.

VCA: Voltage Controlled Amplifier. A device that adjusts the volume of a signal proportionally to the control voltage applied to it.

VCF: Voltage Controlled Filter: A filter whose cut-off frequency is proportional to the voltage applied to it. Some VCFs also provide voltage controllable resonance.

VCO: Voltage Controlled Oscillator: A device generating an output signal of frequency proportional to the voltage applied to it.

Vernier: A scale (measuring device) fixed to potentiometer in place of a knob, which enables that parameter to be set at a particular position with a high degree of accuracy.

Vibrato: See **Frequency Modulation.**

Vocoder: A device that analyses the frequency content of an incoming signal, and uses that information to control a bank of filters that are to process a second signal. In this way, a sound can retain its original pitch yet take on the timbral characteristics of another sound. Alternatively, inanimate sounds can be pitched into a chromatic scale.

Voice Module: The combined forces of oscillators, filter, amplifier, envelope generators, low frequency oscillators, all the blocks that are used to make a synthesized sound can be considered as a whole – a voice module.

Volatile Memory: A memory system that requires a constant power source in order to retain the information in it. If the power fails, the information is permanently lost.

Voltage Control: The basis of operation for most synthesizers. Voltages are used to change parameters as desired. The advantage of this system is that most circuits produce voltages, so one device can be used to control another, and so on.

Voltage Trigger: A type of triggering signal that consists of a fast change in voltage – either positive or negative.

Waveform Modulation: A voltage controlled change in the shape of a given waveform, without any corresponding change in frequency.

Wheel: A form of performance control, normally used for pitchbending or modulation.

White Noise: A random combination of all frequencies in equal amounts over the entire audio spectrum.